2004

W9-BYD-635

Drowning
Our Sorrows
Psychological Effects of Alcohol Abuse

THE ENCYCLOPEDIA OF PSYCHOLOGICAL DISORDERS

Senior Consulting Editor Carol C. Nadelson, M.D.
Consulting Editor Claire E. Reinburg

Drowning
Our Sorrows
Psychological Effects of Alcohol Abuse

Nancy Peacock

CHELSEA HOUSE PUBLISHERS
Philadelphia

The ENCYCLOPEDIA OF PSYCHOLOGICAL DISORDERS provides up-to-date information on the history of, causes and effects of, and treatment and therapies for problems affecting the human mind. The titles in this series are not intended to take the place of the professional advice of a psychiatrist or mental health care professional.

Chelsea House Publishers
Editor in Chief: Stephen Reginald
Managing Editor: James D. Gallagher
Production Manager: Pamela Loos
Art Director: Sara Davis
Director of Photography: Judy L. Hasday

Staff for DROWNING OUR SORROWS: PSYCHOLOGICAL EFFECTS OF ALCOHOL ABUSE
Editorial Assistant: Anne Hill, Heather Forkos
Picture Researcher: Sandy Jones
Associate Art Director: Takeshi Takahashi
Designer: 21st Century Publishing and Communications, Inc.
Cover Designer: Brian Wible

The ChelseaHouse World Wide Web site address is
http://www.chelseahouse.com

First Printing

1 3 5 7 9 8 6 4 2

Library of Congress Cataloging-in-Publication Data

Peacock, Nancy.
Drowning our sorrows : the psychological effects of alcohol abuse / by Nancy Peacock.
p. cm. — (Encyclopedia of psychological disorders)
Includes bibliographical references and index.
Summary: An overview of the psychological damage that alcoholism can cause if left untreated.
ISBN 0-7910-4954-X
1. Alcoholism—United States—Juvenile literature.   2. Alcoholism—United States—Psychological aspects—Juvenile literature.
3. Alcoholism—Treatment—United States—Juvenile literature.
[1. Alcoholism.]   I. Title.   II. Series.
HV5066.P43   1999
362.292—dc21   99-11418
                                                               CIP
                                                               AC

CONTENTS

PSYCHOLOGICAL DISORDERS AND THEIR EFFECT

CAROL C. NADELSON, M.D.
PRESIDENT AND CHIEF EXECUTIVE OFFICER,
The American Psychiatric Press

There are a wide range of problems that are considered psychological disorders, including mental and emotional disorders, problems related to alcohol and drug abuse, and some diseases that cause both emotional and physical symptoms. Psychological disorders often begin in early childhood, but during adolescence we see a sharp increase in the number of people affected by these disorders. It has been estimated that about 20 percent of the U.S. population will have some form of mental disorder sometime during their lifetime. Some psychological disorders appear following severe stress or trauma. Others appear to occur more often in some families and may have a genetic or inherited component. Still other disorders do not seem to be connected to any cause we can yet identify. There has been a great deal of attention paid to learning about the causes and treatments of these disorders, and exciting new research has taught us a great deal in the last few decades.

The fact that many new and successful treatments are available makes it especially important that we reject old prejudices and outmoded ideas that consider mental disorders to be untreatable. If psychological problems are identified early, it is possible to prevent serious consequences. We should not keep these problems hidden or feel shame that we or a member of our family has a mental disorder. Some people believe that something they said or did caused a mental disorder. Some people think that these disorders are "only in your head" so that you could "snap out of it" if you made the effort. This type of thinking implies that a treatment is a matter of willpower or motivation. It is a terrible burden for someone who is suffering to be blamed for their misery, and often people with psychological disorders are not treated compassionately. We hope that the information in this book will teach you about various mental illnesses.

The problems covered in the volumes in the ENCYCLOPEDIA OF PSYCHOLOGICAL DISORDERS were selected because they are of particular importance to young adults, because they affect them directly or because they affect family and friends. There are individual volumes on reading disorders, attention deficit and disruptive behavior disorders, and dementia—all of these are related to our abilities to learn and integrate information from the world around us. There are books on drug abuse that provide useful information about the effects of these drugs and treatments that are available for those individuals who have drug problems. Some of the books concentrate on one of the most common mental disorders, depression. Others deal with eating disorders, which are dangerous illnesses that affect a large number of young adults, especially women.

Most of the public attention paid to these disorders arises from a particular incident involving a celebrity that awakens us to our own vulnerability to psychological problems. These incidents of celebrities or public figures revealing their own psychological problems can also enable us to think about what we can do to prevent and treat these types of problems.

Nearly 20 million people in the United States—1 in every 13 adults—are alcoholics or abuse alcohol, and approximately 53 percent of Americans say that one or more of their close relatives have a drinking problem. Alcohol abuse is the third-leading cause of preventable death in the United States, contributing to 100,000 deaths each year.

ALCOHOLISM: AN OVERVIEW

Alcohol has been a part of human society nearly as long as society has existed. Yet standards concerning the use of alcohol have continued to change over the course of time. The pendulum has swung all the way from Roman society encouraging the abuse of alcohol to some of the world's major religions preaching total abstinence. There even was a 14-year period during the early part of the 20th century when alcohol was illegal in the United States.

In spite of the well-known dangers of alcohol abuse, alcohol remains the most widely used psychoactive drug in the United States. (A psychoactive drug is a substance that affects the brain.) Nearly 20 million Americans abuse alcohol or are alcoholics.

Opinions on the use and abuse of alcohol have always been plentiful. Writers and artists have both celebrated the drug's effects and illustrated the misery and damage caused by alcoholism. However, until recently there was very little solid scientific research on this problem. Today, scientists know that alcoholism is a disease that combines a physical and psychological addiction. These professionals are studying many aspects of alcoholism, including the reasons some people seem to be almost instantly addicted to alcohol and how the drug works on the body's organs and tissues. The goal is to discover the best ways to help alcoholics become—and remain—sober, and to learn what can be done to prevent alcoholism in future generations.

This volume in the ENCYCLOPEDIA OF PSYCHOLOGICAL DISORDERS explains the history, causes, symptoms, and treatment of alcoholism. It also discusses the many problems related to alcohol abuse, such as underage drinking, alcoholism in the workplace, drinking and driving, and the effects of alcoholism on the family.

Alcohol use is pervasive in the United States; approximately 70 percent of Americans drink occasionally and 10 percent drink daily.

DEFINING ALCOHOLISM

The alcoholic is a familiar face in movies, sports, art, literature, and politics. We read about celebrities who seem to have everything our society values—fame, money, thousands of adoring fans—and yet they abuse alcohol or become alcoholics. If these celebrities are fortunate, they can turn their lives around through treatment and rehabilitation. But in spite of state-of-the-art treatment centers and the personal support of family and friends, some of these glamorous people die from alcohol-related accidents, suicides, and overdoses.

And then there's the rest of us. As former U.S. senator George McGovern wrote so eloquently in a memoir about his daughter's death from alcoholism:

> Every day three hundred Americans die quietly of alcoholism. Many of them go unnoticed. Some of them have been out of touch with their families for years. There might be a small news item reporting that the police have found an unidentified body in a park or on a street or in a cheap rooming house—or in a snowbank. These people are usually not the subject of public notice or concern. But each one of them is a precious soul who was once a little girl or boy filled with promise and dreams. They are the silent victims of the nation's number one health problem—alcoholism.

Alcohol is the most widely used psychoactive drug in the United States. Alcohol contributes to 100,000 deaths every year, making it the third leading cause of preventable death in this country. Only tobacco and diet/activity patterns cause more preventable deaths. The disease of alcoholism permeates life in the United States. Nearly 20 million Americans—1 in every 13 adults—are alcoholics or abuse alcohol. Approximately 53 percent of Americans say that one or more of their close relatives have a drinking problem.

If alcohol is so destructive, why does our society tolerate the use of alcohol? To put it simply, we are a nation of alcohol drinkers. About 70 percent of American adults drink occasionally, and 10 percent drink daily. Historian W. J.

Rorabaugh, author of *The Alcoholic Republic: An American Tradition,* explains that Americans have long been among the world's heaviest drinkers. "From colonial times to the present alcohol has been pervasive in American society, though the consumption of particular beverages and patterns of drinking in general have not remained stable," he writes. "The use of alcohol has crossed ethnic, racial, class and gender lines, although some groups have customarily imbibed more than others. Campaigns against excessive use or, indeed, against any use at all have been frequent. None have succeeded for more than a brief moment in quenching America's thirst."

As you will see in the next chapter, the battle to control excessive drinking is as old as human history. What has changed, over the centuries, is the way we define and treat alcoholism. Instead of belittling alcoholics for having bad character or imprisoning alcoholics for breaking laws, we now use the science of medicine and psychology to understand how alcohol affects the body and mind.

WHAT IS ALCOHOL?

Alcohol belongs to a family of chemicals that contain carbon (C) and hydrogen (H) atoms, and hydroxyl groups that consist of a hydrogen atom and an oxygen atom (OH). Ethyl alcohol, or ethanol (C_2H_5OH), is the alcohol substance that is found in beer, wine, or spirits, as well as in cough medicines and sleeping pills.

There are three other common types of alcohol. Methyl alcohol, or methanol (CH_3OH), is also known as wood alcohol. Methanol is volatile, flammable, and a solvent, which means that it can be used to dissolve certain other substances. Ethylene glycol ($C_2H_6O_2$) is a thick liquid that is commonly used in automobile antifreeze. Isopropyl alcohol (C_3H_8O) is better known as rubbing alcohol and is commonly used as a disinfectant or antiseptic. All three of these types of alcohol are poisonous. Another member of the alcohol chemical family is glycerol ($C_3H_8O_3$), used in medicines such as nitroglycerin, paints, and cosmetics. Cholesterol, a fat substance produced by the liver, and Vitamin A are also types of alcohol. This book will look at the effects of ethyl alcohol on a person's body and brain.

DEFINING ALCOHOLISM AND ALCOHOL ABUSE

Is everyone who drinks an alcoholic? No. Many people are able to take a drink occasionally without ever having a problem with alcohol use. However, when a person is unable to stop drinking, and his or her life

U.S. senator George McGovern, with his daughter Terry and wife Eleanor, during his 1972 campaign for president. McGovern wrote a book about alcoholism and its effect on families after his daughter, an alcoholic, froze to death in December 1994 while drunk.

and health are affected in a negative way because of alcohol use, there is a good chance that person suffers from alcoholism.

When it comes to alcohol, the ideal is moderate drinking. But this term may mean different things to different people. In general, moderate drinking does not cause problems for the drinker or for those around him or her. People who limit themselves to an occasional glass of wine or a few beers with friends at a Super Bowl party, are probably moderate drinkers.

SIGNS OF A PROBLEM

To help people identify whether they or someone they know has a drinking problem, a four-part series of questions were included in the NIAAA pamphlet entitled "Alcoholism: Getting the Facts." To help people remember the questions, the first letter of the key word in each question spells the word "CAGE."

1. Have you ever felt you should **C**ut down on your drinking?
2. Have people **A**nnoyed you by criticizing your drinking?
3. Have you ever felt bad or **G**uilty about your drinking?
4. Have you ever had a drink first thing in the morning to steady your nerves or to get rid of a hangover (**E**ye opener)?

One "yes" response indicates a possible alcohol problem. More than one "yes" answer means that an alcohol problem is highly likely. Even if all the responses are "no," a drinking problem may exist if the person has an alcohol-related problem with the law, in a relationship, on the job, or with his or her health.

Source: National Institute on Alcohol Abuse and Alcoholism

Unfortunately, this is a vague definition and not very helpful to those looking for guidelines. The U.S. Department of Agriculture and the U.S. Department of Health and Human Services define moderate drinking as no more than two drinks a day for most men and no more than one drink a day for most women. The reason there are different guidelines for men and women is because, in general, women become more intoxicated than men on the same amount of alcohol. The reasons are purely biological. Women typically are smaller than men and are affected more quickly as the alcohol enters their bloodstream. The stomach tissue of males secretes an enzyme that breaks down alcohol faster than women's bodies can. Also, women have less water and generally a higher fat content in their bodies than do men. Alcohol dissolves easier in water than in fat. As a result, the alcohol remains concentrated in a woman's body, while it is dispersed more quickly through a man's body.

The National Institute on Alcohol Abuse and Alcoholism (NIAAA) was created by the federal government in 1970. The NIAAA conducts and supports 90 percent of the $250 million in biomedical and behavioral research into the effects of alcohol on the human mind and body that is conducted in the United States every year.

The NIAAA defines alcoholism, or alcohol dependence syndrome, as a disease characterized by these four elements:

1. Craving: A strong need, or compulsion, to drink.

2. Loss of control: The frequent inability to stop drinking once a person has begun.

3. Physical dependence: The occurrence of withdrawal symptoms, such as nausea, sweating, shakiness, and anxiety, when alcohol use is stopped after a period of heavy drinking. These symptoms are usually relieved by drinking alcohol or by taking another sedative drug.

4. Tolerance: The need for increasing amounts of alcohol in order to get "high."

Moderate drinking—having an occasional beer on a night out with friends or at a party— can be beneficial. Low levels of alcohol can reduce tension and stress, cause pleasant feelings, and reduce feelings of self-consciousness, and some studies indicate that drinking in moderation decreases the risk of heart disease. However, even low levels of drinking can cause health problems and impair driving skills.

The NIAAA has a second classification for people who abuse alcohol without becoming physically dependent on the drug. Alcohol abuse is defined as a pattern of drinking that is accompanied by one or more of the following situations within a 12-month period:

1. Failure to fulfill major work, school, or home responsibilities.
2. Drinking in situations that are physically dangerous, such as while driving a car or operating machinery.
3. Recurring alcohol-related legal problems, such as being arrested for driving under the influence of alcohol or for physically hurting someone while drunk.
4. Continued drinking despite having ongoing relationship problems that are caused or worsened by the effects of alcohol.

THE BENEFITS AND RISKS OF MODERATION

Research has shown that there are benefits to moderate drinking. Low levels of alcohol can reduce tension and stress, cause pleasant feelings, and reduce feelings of self-consciousness. There also is strong evidence that drinking in moderation decreases the risk of death from coronary artery disease. In the elderly, moderate drinking is reported to improve appetite, mood, and bowel function.

However, relatively low levels of drinking can still cause problems. Moderate drinking increases the potential risk of strokes caused by bleeding, although it decreases the risk of strokes caused by blocked blood vessels. And small amounts of alcohol can significantly impair driving skills, even if the level of the drug in the bloodstream is significantly below the legal definition of intoxication. The act of driving a vehicle requires complex physical coordination and brain function: two areas that are directly affected by alcohol.

Birth defects are associated with low levels of alcohol consumption. Animal research shows that nervous system abnormalities occurred in monkeys whose mothers were given low doses of alcohol. In humans, mothers who reported consuming an average of two to three drinks per day during pregnancy had children who were smaller in weight, length, and head circumference and who had more minor physical anomalies. Mothers who reported as few as two drinks per day during pregnancy had children whose IQ scores were below normal when they were measured at seven years of age.

This woman is drinking while helping her daughter with her homework. One sign of an alcoholic is a craving, or need for the drug.

Some people should not drink any alcohol. Those people include women who are pregnant or trying to become pregnant, people who are planning to drive or do some other activity that requires attention and skill, people taking medications, recovering alcoholics, people under the age of 21, and those with certain medical conditions, such as peptic ulcers.

This illustration from the tomb of an Egyptian pharaoh who lived 3,600 years ago shows men making wine. The group is pressing grapes, while the man at the left collects the juice in jars. Humans have been making alcoholic drinks since before written history.

2

A HISTORY OF ALCOHOL USE

No one really knows when alcohol was first discovered, but the first alcoholic beverage probably was created when airborne yeast combined with a sugary mashed-up food. We know that prehistoric humans began copying the process because 8,000-year-old writings from early civilizations indicate that alcohol was used in ceremonies and festivals, and the recorded legends of these cultures told how the people had been given this "gift" from their ancestors.

The invention of wine is included in an ancient Babylonian myth about the creation of the world. According to the story, there was a struggle over the earth between the forces of good and evil, and many warriors were killed on both sides. When the powers of good finally won the battle, the good warriors who had been killed and had fallen to the earth were transformed into grapevines as a memorial to their sacrifice. The juice from the grapes was made into wine. This story is one of many early religious stories in which wine is portrayed as sacrificial blood.

Another story tells about the discovery of wine in ancient Persia. A Persian king named Jamshid loved grape juice and stored it in large jars. One jar was accidentally exposed to air, allowing fermentation to occur and create wine. The king, believing the juice had spoiled, ordered the jar labeled as poison. One of the king's concubines, who suffered from headaches, decided to kill herself by drinking the poison. When the wine cured her headache instead of killing her, she cajoled the king into trying it. Jamshid began production of this juice and called it *zeher-e-hoosh,* the delightful poison.

Wine was an ingredient in medications that were used in the earliest civilizations, according to records found in Mesopotamia dating back to 6,000 B.C. Early civilizations in China and India also used fermented drinks in medicinal and religious ceremonies. Egyptians drank *hek,* a beer made from barley.

With the development of alcoholic drinks came the problem of alcoholism.

The tomb of an Egyptian king who lived more than 5,000 years ago indicates that abuse of alcohol was a factor in his death. An inscription on the tomb reads, "His earthly abode [meaning his body] was rent and shattered by wine and beer. And the spirit escaped before it was called for."

As soon as societies began establishing standard ways of producing alcoholic beverages, they began to limit the use of alcohol. Over 3,700 years ago, a Babylonian king named Hammurabi established a code of laws to regulate the lives of his subjects. One of the earliest recorded legal codes, the Code of Hammurabi laid out a variety of restrictions on the consumption and sale of alcohol. Violators of these laws could be executed. Similarly, in China during the reign of Emperor Chung K'iang, drunkards were executed to show that the government did not approve of excessive drinking.

The Bible has more than 150 references to alcohol, and these warnings created a cultural taboo against excessive drinking in the Jewish culture. The author of the Old Testament book of Proverbs warns that "Wine is a mocker, strong drink is raging; and whosoever is deceived thereby is not wise."

THE GREEKS AND ROMANS

The ancient Greeks were known for moderate drinking. In the Greek civilization that flourished between 1,000 and 150 B.C., it was considered barbarous to drink wine that was not diluted with water. Greek law called for government wine inspectors and fines for public drunkenness.

Wine was a part of the Greek *symposium,* a large organized gathering where men discussed philosophical ideas. During these discussions, meats and fruits were eaten, and specific amounts of wine, diluted with water, were served. The Greeks believed this carefully regulated eating and drinking enhanced the quality of the discussions.

The theme of moderation even shows up in the cultural writings of the day. Dionysus, the Greek god of wine and fertility, was portrayed as spreading the message of moderation throughout his travels to Thrace and India. In Greek historic tales, the enemy was defeated because of drunkenness. Medical advice included recommendations of moderate drinking.

As Greek society declined and a new power, the Romans, emerged in the fourth and third centuries B.C., all that changed. The Romans were

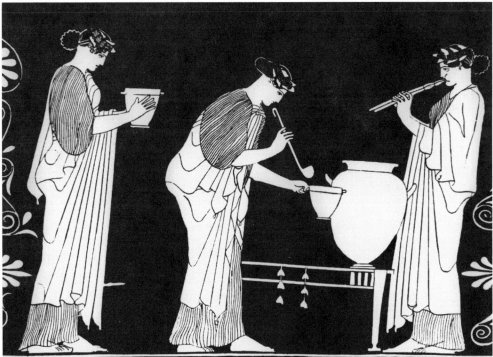

The Greeks used wine in moderation as part of their discussions, or symposiums. *This artwork from a vase shows Greek women diluting wine with water.*

greatly influenced by the Greeks, and the gods in their religion were similar to the Greek pantheon of deities. However, the Roman version of Dionysus, called Bacchus, was much less restrained than his Greek counterpart. Bacchus was known for his excessive drinking and constant reveling. In one Roman myth, recounted in a poem written in the first century B.C., King Midas wins a 10-day drinking contest, and as a reward Bacchus gives Midas the power to turn everything he touches into gold. The Romans adapted other aspects of Greek culture into their civilization, including the symposium. However, the Romans did not practice moderation; instead, their version was an orgy of overeating and excessive drinking.

A Roman emperor named Domitius Ulpinus believed that alcoholism was a disease that would destroy the empire. Eventually, in 186 B.C., the Roman Senate outlawed symposiums. To combat the alcoholism spreading through Roman culture, Domitius ordered half the vineyards in the empire to be destroyed and raised the price of wine. This reduced the problem.

THE WATER OF LIFE

As Christianity replaced the pagan religions of Greece and Rome, the drinking customs of western Europe began to be influenced by the writings of the New Testament, which called for sobriety. However, by the third century, drinking to celebrate the festival days of Christian martyrs was popular.

In the early Middle Ages (A.D. 500–1000), the Germanic tribes of the North drank beer and cider; the people living in the warmer countries of France, Spain, and Italy primarily drank wine; and the inhabitants of the British Isles drank beer and mead (an alcoholic drink made from fermented honey and water). Later, the religious Crusades (1095–1291) helped to improve wine production in Europe. When the European crusaders returned from fighting the Muslims, they brought an unusual grapevine back from Persia. These vines were planted in France, and the combination of the plant and that country's climate resulted in grapes of such quality that wine from France became the world standard.

Distillation of spirits originated in the Greek and Roman civilizations, but this process did not become popular in Europe until about 1250. Around this time, two chemists living in central Europe (the area that today is Switzerland) published personal accounts in which they said that distilled alcohol had enabled both of them to live to age 70. This was a major accomplishment in the Middle Ages, when the average person could only expect to live half that long. This new view of distilled alcohol as medicine quickly gained popularity, and alcohol became known as *aqua vitae*, which is Latin for "water of life." Distilled alcohol was touted as a cure for colds, baldness, jaundice, and deafness, and it was considered a way to improve memory and give courage.

The distillation process is simple. Alcohol boils at a lower temperature than water. A fermented mash of grains, containing perhaps 14 to 20 percent alcohol, was cooked over a carefully tended fire. The heat would have to be low enough to keep the water in the mixture from boiling, but high enough to cause the alcohol to condense into vapor. The alcohol vapor would rise from the mixture, separating from the water and nonalcoholic portion. Instead of allowing it to escape into the

Unlike the Greeks, Romans did not practice moderation in drinking. Their celebrations and religious rituals usually involved heavy drinking and wild singing and dancing. The Latin word for these celebrations, orgia, *is the root of the English word "orgy," meaning drunken revelry.*

air, however, the alcohol vapor was trapped and cooled. This condenses it into liquid again. Distilled alcohol is more concentrated—typically 70 to 90 percent alcohol—and therefore more potent. But making the drink more potent required new laws to stem the tide of increased drunkenness. By the end of the 13th century, both Switzerland and England had introduced laws requiring taverns that served alcohol to close by a certain time.

In the Middle Ages, distilled alcohol was known as aqua vitae, *or "water of life." It was often used as medicine, and was believed to increase a person's lifespan. However, this woodcut illustrates the effects of alcohol abuse.*

In 1496, Germany passed the first laws to prohibit the sale of alcohol on Sundays and other religious holidays. Germans also started the first temperance societies. Unlike societies or religions that banned all alcohol, the concept of temperance emphasized drinking moderately.

Franciscus Sylvius, a Dutch chemist, discovered a method for distilling alcohol that created a potent medicine with a raw taste. He flavored it with juniper, and soon the medicine was a popular drink. The French word for the juniper flavoring was *genievre,* which the English shortened to "gin." A similar process became popular in Russia; there, the resulting drink, made from potatoes or grain, was called vodka.

Because of the abundance and quality of grapes grown in France, wine was the prefered drink, and drinking distilled grain never became as popular as it was in the British Isles and other European nations. In

1690, the English government passed the Act for Encouraging the Distillation of Brandy and Spirits from Corn. Four years after the law was enacted, a million gallons of gin had been distilled. By 1742, English distillers were selling 20 million gallons a year. In order to control the amount of alcohol while making money from its sale, the English government began taxing all alcohol created for drinking. "Denatured" alcohol, or alcohol that was poisoned so that it could not be drunk, was the only alcohol not taxed by the 1743 laws.

Although the laws on alcohol were passed to help British business interests, the damaging effects of excessive drinking soon became a problem in the British Isles. As drinking became more widespread, English art and literature began portraying the damage done by alcohol. Novels by Charles Dickens are full of characters whose lives are ruined by drunkenness, and illustrator William Hogarth portrayed the human misery of alcohol in drawings entitled "Gin Lane" and "Beer Street."

ALCOHOL IN THE NEW WORLD

The Caribbean islands discovered by Christopher Columbus, called the West Indies, offered a plentiful supply of molasses. It wasn't long before European colonists in the New World created "rumbullion," or rum, from fermented molasses. The molasses was distilled into rum in the early European colonies in North America, and soon a trade triangle formed: the New England distillers shipped rum to Africa, where it was exchanged for slaves; the slaves were traded in the West Indies for molasses; then the molasses was shipped north to the New England distillers to create more rum. Because there were no taxes on this trade triangle, profits were high and rum was cheap. Rum became a favorite alcoholic drink in Colonial America.

The early European colonists also attempted to trade with the Natives Americans. Alcohol was not a part of everyday Native American culture, so Europeans used liquor as an underhanded bargaining tool. The traders would encourage the chief to drink until he was thoroughly drunk. Because the Native American chiefs had little experience with alcohol, the drug would confuse them during treaty negotiations.

In colonial America, people of all ages drank beer with their meals. Housewives brewed the family's beer supply once or twice a week. Hard apple cider was one of the most common alcoholic beverages in the 1700s. In the south, farmers also fermented and drank peach cider, called "peachy."

Dr. Benjamin Rush (1746–1813) was one of the leading physicians of his day. A colonial patriot, he was a signer of the Declaration of Independence, and served as physician general for the Continental Army from 1776–78, writing a pioneering book on military medical care. After the Revolutionary War, Rush advocated moderation in drinking; his beliefs led to the temperance movement in the United States.

In New England, the Puritans enjoyed hard liquor in moderation, believing it gave a person strength, health, and good digestion. But public drunkenness was not tolerated. Taverns were licensed, and only church members of good character were granted licenses. Clergymen monitored taverns to ensure that no one spent too much time drinking, and lists were posted of people who were banned from buying alcohol.

In the south, excessive drinking was more common. Political candidates bought voters drinks on election day. In 1755, George Washington lost an election in the Virginia House of Burgesses because he did not treat the voters to alcohol, and Virginia governor William Byrd later recorded in his diary that members of his Governor's Council became drunk at council meetings.

By the time of the American Revolution, the 13 colonies produced enough grain to make whiskey cheaply. This marked the beginning of the end for the rum trade. During the Revolution, the English blockaded Atlantic seaports, cutting off the supply of rum and molasses to American distillers. After the end of the war, whiskeys made from corn and rye became popular. In Pennsylvania, farmers discovered they could make more money by distilling and selling rye whiskey than by shipping the grain to market. When the government tried to tax the whiskey, the farmers revolted. The Whiskey Rebellion of 1794 was put down by the government, but the whiskey business continued to prosper. In 1808, the U.S. Congress abolished the slave trade; this broke the trade triangle and further reduced the market for rum.

In the early 19th century, almost all Americans drank whiskey. The average adult drank seven gallons of distilled alcohol per year—nearly three times today's consumption levels. In *The Alcoholic Republic: An American Tradition*, W. J. Rorabaugh described drinking in the early 1800s:

> Children were given liquor as soon as they were old enough to lift a glass. Teenagers swaggered into taverns and, pretending to be adults, ordered whiskey. Men and women commonly indulged, and a grandmother who declined a glass might be thought to be ailing.
>
> Americans drank throughout the day. An American commonly arose with an "eye-opener" before breakfast, downed a whiskey with breakfast, and adjourned at 11 a.m. from the farm, shop or business for a whisky break, the predecessor of a coffee break. Mid-afternoon dinner brought another glass, followed by a whisky break in afternoon, liquor with supper and a nightcap.

THE TEMPERANCE MOVEMENT

Toward the end of the 18th century, a Philadelphia physician named Benjamin Rush began studying the negative effects of alcohol. He believed that alcoholism was a disease, and he studied the damage to the body caused by excessive drinking. In 1784, he published an essay titled *An Enquiry into the Effects of Spiritous Liquors upon the Human Body, and their Influence upon the Happiness of Society*. In his pamphlet, Rush advocated moderation in drinking and warned people that too much hard liquor would ruin their health. He also proposed heavy taxes on liquor, a limit on the number of taverns in each city, and harsh penalties for public drunkenness.

Rush's beliefs formed the basis of the "temperance" movement in the United States during the 1820s and 1830s. In a reaction against excessive drinking, members of the clergy began preaching against alcohol as a "tool of the devil." By 1830, the American Temperance Society had 1,000 local chapters. Between 1825 and 1840 millions of people stopped or reduced their drinking, and by 1849, the consumption of distilled alcohol had fallen by 75 percent. The temperance movement continued through the rest of the 19th century, although drinking levels rose slightly during the Civil War.

In the 20th century, World War I caused a limitation of alcohol use in the United States. Because of food shortages during the war, the Lever Act of 1917 prohibited the use of grain for manufacturing alcoholic beverages. Also, there were still many advocates of temperance, and a national dislike of foreigners, especially the people of nations that were warring with America's allies (Germans were associated with beer drinking, Italians with wine), contributed toward changing people's attitudes. By 1918, state and local laws made large parts of the country, particularly rural areas, "dry." Dry areas prohibited the manufacture and distribution of alcohol.

THE NOBLE EXPERIMENT: PROHIBITION

In 1919, the 18th Amendment to the Constitution was ratified. It prohibited the manufacture, sale, and transportation of alcohol in the United States. The federal government then passed the Volstead Act to enforce the amendment, making it illegal to drink any beverage with more than 0.5 percent alcohol. (Beer, the beverage with the lowest alcohol content, typically has between 3 and 7 percent alcohol.) This begun the 14-year period in U.S. history known as "Prohibition."

Herbert Hoover, later president of the United States, called Prohibition an "experiment noble in purpose." The government ban on alcohol was a dramatic response to the problem of alcoholism in the United States, and it did accomplish some notable results. In the period before the war, the national consumption of alcohol was 2.6 gallons per person; by the early 1930s, it had fallen to under one gallon per person. Arrests for drunkenness and deaths related to alcohol fell off sharply.

However, Prohibition created as many problems as it solved. The government-regulated alcohol industry was replaced with an underground illegal system. The Prohibition Bureau had fewer than 3,000 agents, and smuggling alcohol became a major business. Organized crime took over the lucrative business of making and selling alcohol. The police in many of the country's large cities were paid off by criminals to ignore and protect illegal alcohol manufacture and sale.

People with money who wanted to drink had little trouble finding alcohol. Thousands of illegal bars sprang up across the country, especially

An illegal alcohol "still," used to distill gin, that was discovered by federal agents in Washington, D.C., in 1922, during Prohibition. With the manufacture and sale of alcohol against the law, many people continued making and selling "bootleg" alcohol.

in the cities. These establishments, called "speakeasies" because the people in them would have to "speak easy" in order not to be detected, often bribed members of the local police to overlook their illegal activities.

When Prohibition ended in 1933, the country was in the depths of a terrible worldwide economic slump called the Great Depression. Banks had collapsed, jobs were scarce, and drought had turned some of the western states into "dustbowls." There were more than enough reasons for people to abuse alcohol, and thousands of people did so.

It was not until the 1930s that effective treatment for alcoholism was developed. Since then, groups like Alcoholics Anonymous have helped thousands of problem drinkers put down their glasses for good.

HELP FOR ALCOHOLICS

In 1935, an Akron, Ohio, surgeon named Dr. Bob Smith met a New York stockbroker named Bill Wilson. Both men were alcoholics, but Wilson had stopped drinking and then remained sober by working with other alcoholics. Wilson explained to Smith the spiritual approach that he had used to end his addiction to alcohol; this helped the surgeon to end his own dependence on the drug.

Wilson and Smith began working with other alcoholics at Akron City Hospital. One of their patients became sober; he joined Wilson and Smith in their work, and the three founded a group that would later be called Alcoholics Anonymous. In the fall of that same year, a second group of alcoholics in New York became sober, using the same philosophy and methods.

In 1939, a third fellowship had formed in Cleveland; together the three groups were responsible for helping 100 alcoholics become and remain sober. Bill wrote the Alcoholics Anonymous textbook, which explained the basic Twelve Steps of recovery and included stories of 30 recovered alcoholics. A local newspaper, the *Cleveland Plain Dealer*, published a series of articles about the organization, and within a few months the membership of the Cleveland chapter went from 20 to 500.

The Alcoholics Anonymous philosophy and methods demonstrated for the first time that sobriety could be accomplished by a large number of people. By 1950, 100,000 alcoholics worldwide had used the philosophy of Alcoholics Anonymous to become sober.

In 1944, a woman named Marty Mann became the first woman to find sobriety in the Alcoholics Anonymous program. Her goal became spreading the word that alcoholism is a disease and that the alcoholic is a sick person. With one secretary and a small office, she started the National Committee for Education on Alcohol. That organization is known today as the National Council on Alcoholism and Drug Dependence (NCADD).

By setting up community organizations that would operate information centers, Mann's NCADD was able to convince many in the medical community as well as the public of the alcoholism-as-disease concept. When Mann founded the NCADD, fewer than 100 general hospitals accepted acute alcoholism cases. By 1953, 3,000 hospitals offered this care. In a 1943 opinion poll, 6 percent of the population thought alcoholism was a disease. By 1957, that number had jumped to 58 percent.

In 1950, Lois Wilson, the wife of Bill Wilson, founded Al-Anon for the families and friends of alcoholics. Al-Anon was created by and for people affected by alcoholism. They had the need to share their experience, strength, and hope with others who were enduring the same problems in order to solve those problems. In 1957, a teenage boy whose parents were involved in AA/Al-Anon in California started the first Alateen group for teens dealing with alcoholic relatives and friends. Since then, Alateen has expanded to include preteen family members.

SCIENTIFIC RESEARCH INTO ALCOHOLISM BEGINS

The success of AA had demonstrated that recovery from alcoholism was possible on a large scale. At the same time, scientists conducted the first modern studies of alcoholism as a disease. This led to the establishment of the Research Council on Problems of Alcohol at Yale University in the mid-1930s. Then in 1940 the *Quarterly Journal of Studies on Alcohol* began publishing articles that focused on a scientific approach to alcoholism. This journal was instrumental in portraying alcoholism as a disease with a scientific solution.

Others joined in the fight to educate the public and further scientific research. The National Council on Alcohol and Drug Dependence, founded by Marty Mann in 1944, was created to educate the public about alcoholism. It still serves as an information clearinghouse for alcoholism treatment and counseling services.

By the 1950s, the medical establishment had begun to be involved in the health care aspects of alcoholism. The American Medical Association and the World Health Organization addressed the discrimination against alcoholics in hospitals and other medical settings. In 1956, the American Medical Association passed a resolution calling for alcoholism to be accepted for treatment in general hospitals. The following year, the American Hospital Association passed a resolution to help prevent discrimination against alcoholics.

In the next decade the American Psychiatric Association and the American Public Health Association joined the supporters of alcoholism as an illness. The U.S. Public Health Service had begun a small program for grants in alcohol research through the National Institute of Mental Health (NIMH). This led the NIMH to establish the National Center for the Prevention and Control of Alcohol Problems in 1965, but the limited research money was inadequate for studying a problem of this magnitude.

To find a way to address alcoholism at a comprehensive national level, many alcohol-related organizations joined forces in 1968. They found a champion for this legislation in senator Harold Hughes, a former governor of Iowa in his first term as a U.S. senator and a recovering alcoholic. In 14 hearings across the country, Hughes served as chairman of the Special Subcommittee on Alcoholism and Narcotics. During the summer of 1969, the committee gathered testimony about the need to establish a federal program for alcohol research.

The following year, the bill, called the Comprehensive Alcohol Abuse and Alcoholism Prevention Treatment and Rehabilitation Act, was passed unanimously by the Senate. The legislation squeezed through the House of Representatives just before the end of the 1970 session. Even though President Nixon's advisors opposed the legislation, he was persuaded by its proponents to sign the bill quietly on the last day of 1970.

This historic legislation is sometimes called alcoholism's Magna Carta because it established personal rights for the alcoholic. It required that records of alcoholic patients be kept confidential and prohibited discrimination against alcoholics in the workplace. In addition, the new law created the National Institute of Alcoholism and Alcohol Abuse (NIAAA), a national agency to develop alcohol research. Since then, NIAAA has coordinated alcohol research and established a body of scientific information that has brought about a greater understanding of alcoholism and addiction in general.

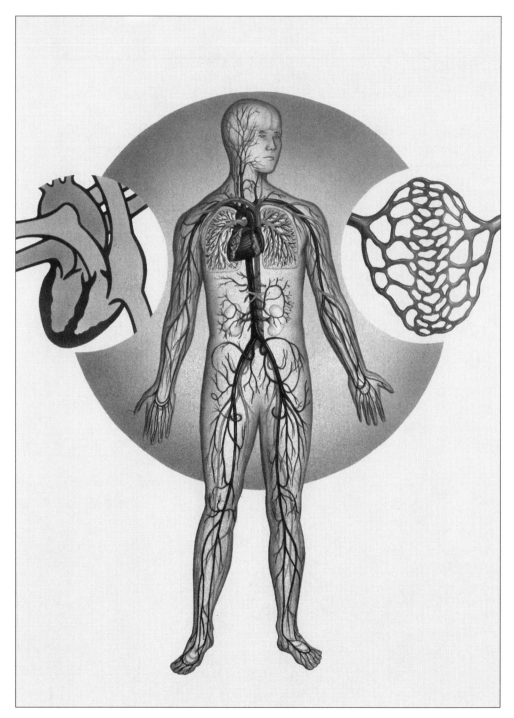

A view of the human circulatory system. When a person drinks, most of the alcohol enters the bloodstream, which distributes it throughout the body.

3

ALCOHOL AND THE HUMAN BODY

W hat happens in the human body when a person consumes alcohol? While the person is ingesting the alcohol, his or her body is simultaneously working hard to rid itself of the drug. A small percentage of the alcohol (about 5 percent) can be eliminated by the body through urine, but the digestive system must process and eliminate the remaining portion of the drug.

When any food or drink enters the body, it is broken down in the stomach into compounds that can be used by the body. This process is called metabolism. These compounds pass through the stomach and intestines into the blood stream, and from there throughout the body. In the liver, a metabolic process called oxidation takes place. This removes toxins from the blood.

When alcohol is ingested, enzymes (body chemicals that the stomach uses to break down other chemicals) begin to work on the alcohol. The enzyme called alcohol dehydrogenase (ADH) converts alcohol to a substance called acetaldehyde (CH_2CHO). However, a second enzyme is needed to break down this substance because acetaldehyde is very toxic. This enzyme changes acetaldehyde to acetic acid, which the body can metabolize into carbon dioxide and water.

For some reason, men have more ADH in the lining of their stomachs than do women, so women pass on more alcohol straight to the small intestine. This may explain why women have higher blood levels of alcohol than men do after drinking the same amount.

However, only a very small amount of the alcohol is metabolized in the stomach. Most of the alcohol passes through the digestive system and enters the bloodstream, where it is eventually metabolized in the liver.

Alcohol is absorbed into the bloodstream at a faster rate than it can be removed from a person's system. No matter how much alcohol is consumed, the liver can only break down a certain amount of alcohol per hour. A general

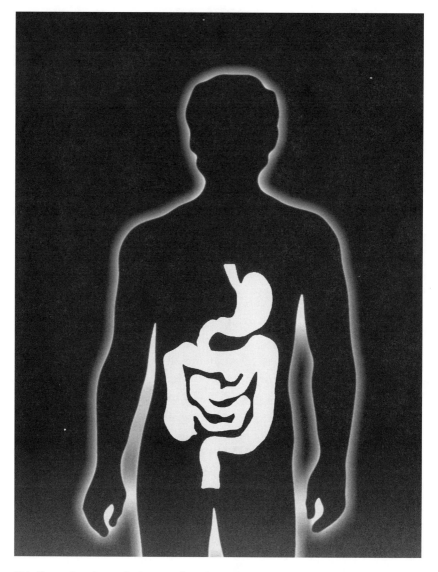

This illustration shows the human digestive system, where the process of metaboliz-
ing alcohol begins. Stomach enzymes convert alcohol to a toxic substance called
acetaldehyde, and then to acetic acid, which the body can expel as carbon dioxide
and water.

rule of thumb is that one standard drink requires 30 to 45 minutes
before the process of metabolism begins to purge the alcohol from the
system. A standard drink is about two-thirds of an ounce—the amount

of alcohol found in a 12-ounce glass of beer, five ounces of wine, or a "shot" (1.5 ounces) of 80-proof distilled spirits.

The level of alcohol in the bloodstream is measured as the percentage of grams of alcohol per milliliter of blood. This is called blood-alcohol concentration, or BAC. When police officers stop a driver that they suspect of driving while intoxicated, they may either test the driver's BAC with an electronic device, called a breathalyzer, that analyzes the amount of alcohol in the person's breath and calculates the BAC, or they may take the driver to a hospital for a blood test to determine BAC. In most states, it is illegal to drive with a BAC over .10 percent, although studies have shown that a BAC as low as .01 percent can affect brain function. A BAC of .30 percent or higher is extremely dangerous; coma or death could result.

TOLERANCE

After a few drinks, a person who abuses alcohol may seem less affected than someone who does not drink regularly. This is because the abuser's body has adapted to the alcohol. As a result, the drinker needs greater amounts of alcohol to produce the same feeling of intoxication. This is called tolerance, because the drinker's body has become tolerant of the drug. There are several different types of alcohol tolerance: functional, metabolic, acute, and environment-dependent.

Functional tolerance develops when the brain changes to compensate for the disruption caused by alcohol. This is indicated when a chronic drinker has a blood-alcohol concentration that would be incapacitating, or even fatal, to another person, yet does not seem intoxicated.

Unlike functional tolerance, metabolic tolerance is the physical ability to eliminate alcohol from the body at a rapid rate. Metabolic tolerance is caused by liver enzymes that increase the breakdown of alcohol in the body. These enzymes are activated by chronic drinking. These enzymes also cause other medications to break down, including diabetes medications and medicine that prevent blood clotting. The enzymes also cause sedatives to break down, increasing tolerance to them and increasing the risk of accidental overdose. Some over-the-counter painkillers such as acetaminophen are broken down by liver enzymes into substances that are toxic to the liver. This can create liver damage in chronic drinkers.

Acute tolerance means that alcohol-induced impairment is greater soon after beginning to drink than later in the drinking session, even though BAC levels are the same at both times. If acute tolerance develops

A person who drinks regularly may develop a tolerance to alcohol. This is because his or her body has become used to the drug, and requires greater amounts to achieve the same feelings of intoxication.

to the feeling of being intoxicated, this may prompt the drinker to drink more alcohol. If the intoxicated feeling is less than the impaired performance of intoxication, this may cause a person to believe that they are capable of driving or performing some other skill that they are not capable of performing.

Environment-dependent tolerance means that a person can drink a greater amount before feeling intoxicated in certain settings than in other situations. This tolerance develops even in social drinkers. In one study, people were given alcohol in an office setting, then asked to perform a hand-eye coordination task. Later, the test was repeated, but the alcohol was provided in a bar. Most of the people performed the task better when drinking in the barroom. This suggests that a bar contains cues, or symbols, that are associated with alcohol and promote environmental tolerance.

Health care professionals point out that people who have a high tolerance to alcohol may be drinking at rates that will place them at risk for medical complications from alcohol, including alcoholism. A genetic predisposition for tolerance may increase the risk for alcoholism.

WITHDRAWAL

A problem called withdrawal occurs when a person's body has become so used to a drug that it adapts chemically, becoming physically dependent on the drug. When that person stops taking the drug and amounts of the substance in the body decline, unpleasant symptoms occur. These can be both mental and physical and may include severe muscle cramps, nausea, convulsions, depression, irritability, and hallucinations. The symptoms of withdrawal can be so unpleasant that the user will continue to drink just to avoid them.

The reason people suffer from these symptoms is that the body is experiencing a reversal of alcohol's effects on the central nervous system. Withdrawal also increases the production of adrenal hormones that can be toxic to nerve cells. The hormones can also damage a part of the brain called the hippocampus, which is thought to be important for memory and control of activity.

Alcohol withdrawal has mild to more serious forms, depending on the person and the level of dependence on alcohol. In the milder form, a person can experience shaking, seizures, and hallucinations within 6 to 48 hours after his or her last drink. In the more serious form, a person experiences delirium tremens, or "the d.t.'s," a severe nervous system

DRINKING AND DRIVING

The list of alcohol-related driving impairments is a lengthy one. Alcohol-impaired drivers need more time to read a street sign or respond to a traffic signal than do unimpaired drivers, so impaired drivers respond by looking for fewer sources of information. This narrowing of attention begins to occur at low BAC levels.

The brain controls eye movements, and that process is very vulnerable to the effects of alcohol. The brain is also impaired in its psychomotor skills that involve eye-brain-hand coordination. This is especially important when operating any type of vehicle. The process of driving requires the eyes to focus briefly on certain objects and track them as they move. Even low and moderate levels of blood alcohol concentration (BAC) interfere with the eye's ability to track a moving object.

Another important aspect of driving is the act of steering. This complex psychomotor task requires eye-to-hand reaction time coupled with the eye's ability to follow objects in a visual field. Again, even a low BAC significantly impairs a person's ability to steer.

Drinking and driving is one of the most important problems related to alcohol abuse. Thousands of people die each year in alcohol-related auto accidents.

One of the most critical parts of driving is the ability to divide attention among all the necessary skills. For example, driving a car means paying equal attention to monitoring the location of other vehicles and pedestrians, reading traffic signals, and keeping the vehicle in the proper lane while going in the right direction. What happens to alcohol-impaired drivers is that instead of being able to monitor all aspects of driving equally, they tend to pay more attention to one task than another. So they may pay too much attention to steering and not enough to reading traffic signals.

Even though law enforcement measures BACs or breath alcohol as a means to establish legal limits for drunkenness, alcohol-related impairment of the brain occurs at the lowest measurable alcohol levels. Or as a current advertising campaign against drinking and driving puts it, "Impairment begins with the first drink."

overactivity marked by profound confusion and hallucinations. If untreated, delirium tremens can be fatal about 20 percent of the time.

ALCOHOL'S EFFECTS ON THE BRAIN

Research verifies what history has already shown us: alcohol adversely affects the functioning of the brain. Alcohol impairs nearly every aspect of information processing, or cognitive skills, by the brain.

Alcohol has a depressing effect on the central nervous system; this means that it slows the functions controlled by the brain. Alcohol reduces the ability of nerve cells, called neurons, to produce and transmit electrical signals, or impulses, from the brain to different parts of the body, and from the body to the brain. This reduces the amount of information the brain receives and sends to the body. Thinking, judgment, motor skills, and reactions are all affected.

At low levels, alcohol causes a slight increase in heart and respiration rates while slightly depressing brain function. People drinking usually feel a mild sense of elation, relaxation, and pleasure. Their judgment may be impaired, and they may be willing to do things they would not ordinarily do.

As a person ingests more alcohol, the drug has a depressant effect on nearly all physical systems. This is marked by a dramatic increase in reaction time, impairment of balance and movement, slurred speech, and possibly increased feelings of anxiety or depression. The drinker may become physically sick and vomit, or he or she may "pass out," or fall asleep.

A person who continues drinking and has a BAC of .16 percent or higher suffers from a severe reduction in their awareness of what is happening around them, as well as severe motor impairment (for example, staggering or falling). At a BAC of .30 percent, the drinker may lose consciousness or fall into a coma. Reaching or exceeding this BAC level can be fatal.

LONG-TERM EFFECTS ON THE BRAIN

By the time most alcoholics enter treatment, there is measurable damage to their brain functions. In neuropsychological testing, about 45 to 70 percent of alcoholics have specific deficits in problem solving, abstract thinking, concept shifting, psychomotor performance, or difficult memory tasks. Studies report that the brains of alcoholics can undergo structural changes as well as altered brainwave activity and reduced blood flow through the brain.

In more severe cases of alcoholism, serious organic cerebral impairment occurs in about 10 percent of the cases. Even after alcoholics stop drinking, severe brain dysfunction can continue. Alcoholics can suffer from one of two disorders. Alcohol amnestic disorder, also known as Korsakoff's psychosis or Wernicke-Korsakoff syndrome, is described as short-term memory impairment and behavioral changes that occur without clouding of consciousness or general loss of intellectual abilities. The second disorder, dementia associated with alcoholism, is a global loss of intellectual abilities with an impairment in memory function, disturbances of abstract thinking, judgment, other higher critical functions or personality change without a clouding of consciousness.

Alcohol-related impairment may occur for a number of reasons. One of the direct and most obvious reasons is the toxicity of alcohol itself. Another indirect reason might be that alcohol abuse has caused physical trauma or poor nutritional habits. Some cognitive impairments may be the result of liver disease while other alcoholics may have been impaired before they began drinking.

There is even research that suggests that alcohol has the same effect on cognition as premature aging. Some alcoholics' cognitive deficits resemble those seen in elderly persons who are not alcoholic.

Evidence suggests that some of the alcohol-related impairment is reversible. When alcoholics stop drinking, researchers report that there is some apparent recovery of cognitive function. This may be due to the absence of alcohol, better nutrition, or increased social interaction. Some evidence shows that remedial mental exercises and cognitive training can bring about recovery from alcohol-related impairment.

ALCOHOL AND THE LIVER

While the brain is the organ most obviously affected by alcohol, the liver is the largest organ in the body and experiences the brunt of alcoholic damage. Alcoholic liver disease is one of the most serious medical consequences of alcohol abuse. Alcohol is the most important cause of liver disease and death in the United States.

The liver is a busy and essential organ. It filters the blood stream by removing and destroying toxins. The liver secretes bile into the small

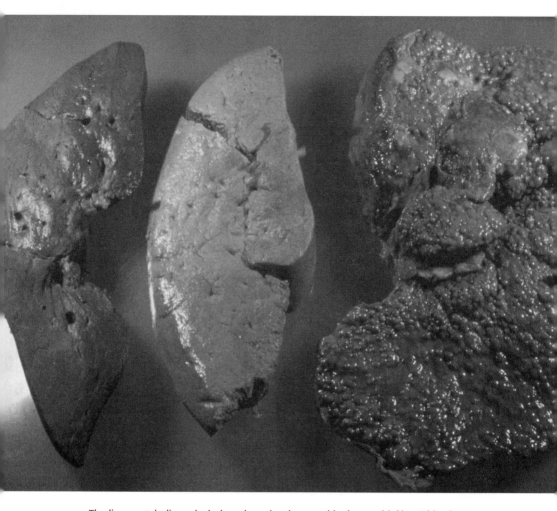

The liver metabolizes alcohol, and can be damaged by heavy drinking. This picture compares a normal liver (left), a fatty liver (center), and a cirrhotic liver (right).

intestine to digest and absorb fats and works with the other metabolic systems in the body.

The liver regulates blood clotting and blood fluidity. It converts the metabolized protein into urea for excretion by the kidneys. The liver stores vitamins, synthesizes cholesterol, metabolizes or stores sugar, and assembles amino acids into various proteins. The body must have a normally functioning liver in order to live.

Alcohol can cause three liver conditions, two of which are life threatening. The first is a rapid increase in fat found in the liver and blood. Almost all heavy drinkers show signs of fatty liver. This is caused by the oxidation of alcohol in addition to any fatty food eaten. The fat goes away soon after a person stops drinking, and fatty liver rarely causes illness. Researchers are unsure of the harm caused by fatty liver.

Evidence of permanent damage is more visible with severe alcoholic hepatitis, an inflammation of the liver. Between 10 and 35 percent of heavy drinkers develop alcoholic hepatitis. This hepatitis results in fever, jaundice, and abdominal pain and can be confused with other serious abdominal conditions, such as inflammation of the pancreas, appendix, and gall bladder.

The most severe form of alcoholic liver injury is alcoholic cirrhosis. Researchers do not know how alcohol causes cirrhosis. Cirrhosis is a disease of the liver in which healthy cells are destroyed and replaced with scar tissue. Scar tissue closes off blood vessels and changes the normal structure of the liver. The most common cause of cirrhosis is alcohol abuse, but it can also be caused by severe hepatitis. Alcoholic cirrhosis can appear with little warning, and death can occur during the early weeks of treatment.

If the alcoholic survives the early onset of cirrhosis and lives long enough to leave treatment, abstinence is the only way to maintain long-term survival. In one study 80 percent of those who had stopped drinking altogether or had greatly reduced drinking were alive seven years later. Only 50 percent of those who continued to drink were alive seven years later.

Liver transplants are the only effective treatment for terminally ill patients. This procedure has been as successful in alcoholic cirrhotic patients as in nonalcoholic cirrhotic patients.

Alcoholics may have one or all three of the alcohol-related liver conditions. Abstinence can reverse the effects of fatty liver and alcoholic hepatitis. Abstinence can stabilize cirrhosis, although the disease is often progressive and fatal.

Complications of liver disease include severe bleeding from distended veins in the esophagus, kidney failure, the accumulation of fluid in the abdomen, and brain disorders.

ALCOHOL AND NUTRITION

Nutritional deficiencies may seem like the least of an alcoholic's problems, but alcohol can cause severe, long-term damage by harming the way the body digests and uses food.

Eating provides energy for the body, nutritional components needed for body function, and replacement of worn-out cells. Many alcoholics neglect eating in favor of drinking. Some alcoholics get as much as 50 percent of their calories from alcohol.

Even if an alcoholic does eat a healthy diet, alcohol interferes with how the body processes food. Alcohol damages the digestive system, compromising the digestion, storage, use, and excretion of nutrients. Food must be digested in order for it to be used. Alcohol inhibits the breakdown of nutrients into usable molecules. It does this by decreasing the secretion of digestive enzymes from the pancreas and damaging the cells lining the stomach and intestines.

The nutrients that do get digested and absorbed may not be fully used by the body. A damaged liver is not able to store adequate amounts of vitamins. Vitamins A, C, D, E, K, and the B vitamins are all involved in maintaining cells and healing wounds. Vitamin K is necessary for blood clotting. Without adequate amounts of vitamin K, alcoholics suffer delayed clotting and excessive bleeding.

Alcohol also impairs the way the body controls blood glucose levels. Glucose is important because it is the body's main source of energy. When a malnourished person drinks alcohol, a chain reaction of hypoglycemia can occur. The body has no food to supply energy, and the stored glucose becomes depleted. Alcohol metabolism inhibits the formation of glucose from other compounds such as amino acids. The body is left with no way to supply energy. The brain and other body tissues are deprived of energy to function. Even brief periods of low glucose levels can cause brain damage.

GENERAL EFFECTS ON THE BODY

Just as alcohol damages the digestive system necessary for the body's nutrition, alcohol interferes with the body's hormones. Hormones are important because they control and coordinate the functions of all the tissue and organs in the body.

Hormones are released from glands throughout the body and sent to

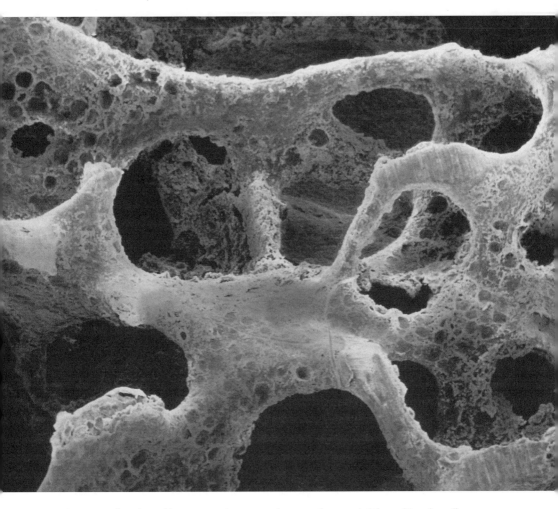

Osteoporosis, a loss of bone mass that causes bones to become brittle and break easily, can occur with heavy alcohol intake. This electron-microscope photograph shows hollow areas of a bone from a person's vertebra.

specific tissues. For glands to do their jobs correctly, the amount and timing from the glands and the response from the tissues must be coordinated and finely tuned. Alcohol can impair those processes, resulting in serious health problems.

Hormones maintain a constant concentration of glucose in the blood. Because alcohol interferes with glucose levels and also with the hormone's actions, binge drinking can cause severe hypoglycemia 6 to 36 hours afterwards.

Alcohol can be especially harmful to people with diabetes because of the predisposition to hypoglycemia. Alcohol consumption can change the effectiveness of hypoglycemic medications. Treatment of diabetes through tight control of glucose levels is difficult with alcoholics because they can experience both hypoglycemic and hyperglycemic (too much glucose) episodes as a result of binge drinking.

The reproductive hormones also suffer from the effects of alcohol. In men, alcohol is directly toxic to the testes and causes reduced testosterone levels. Long-term testosterone deficiency can contribute to breast enlargement and other feminine characteristics.

Alcohol can also interfere with sperm structure and movement. Metabolism of vitamin A is essential to sperm development.

Alcohol can cause many reproductive problems in premenopausal women. Even social drinking levels increase the risk of spontaneous abortion, early menopause, irregular or stopped menstruation, and menstruation without ovulation.

However, in postmenopausal women, alcohol can have a positive effect on some hormones. Women who take three to six drinks a week show an increase in the conversion of testosterone to estradiol. This hormonal conversion is helpful to postmenopausal women and may reduce the risk of cardiovascular disease without increasing the risk of alcoholic liver disease or breast cancer.

Alcohol use can even affect the body's bone structure because it damages or destroys bone-forming cells. Calcium determines the strength and stiffness of the bones. The main storage of calcium is in the bones and teeth, with the rest of the calcium stored in body fluids. Calcium does other important jobs in the body, including facilitating how cells communicate with each other. Hormones control the absorption, excretion, and distribution of calcium. Osteoporosis, a loss of bone mass, is an increased risk for alcoholics. Because alcohol contributes to falling down and bone fractures, the negative effect of alcohol on bone structure is a serious health problem.

ALCOHOL AND PREGNANCY

When alcohol is absorbed, it is distributed to all body fluids. In pregnant women, this includes those fluids in the placenta that nourish the developing fetus. This exposes the unborn child to alcohol. The fetus can

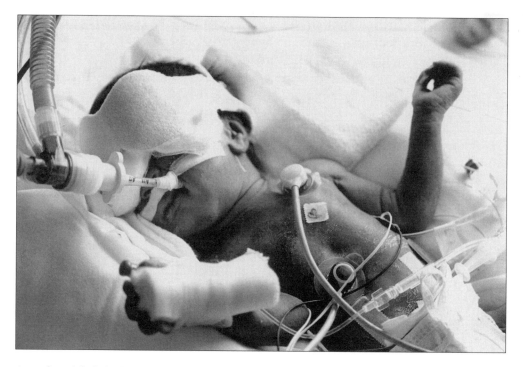

An underweight baby fights for life in a Chicago hospital. Low birth weight, mental retardation, and a host of other physical abnormalities are common when pregnant women drink alcohol. These problems are known collectively as fetal alcohol syndrome.

suffer far greater consequences than the mother from this exposure because the mother's body is more able to rid itself of alcohol's toxins. The drug's impact on the development of the child can be severe. Women who drink alcohol during pregnancy are more likely to have miscarriages, premature deliveries, or stillbirths than those women who abstain from drinking while they are pregnant.

Prenatal alcohol exposure is one of the leading causes of mental retardation. In 1973, the term "fetal alcohol ayndrome" (FAS) was created to describe a pattern of abnormalities in children born to alcoholic mothers. Children with fetal alcohol syndrome may have problems with their central nervous system, such as mental retardation, undersized head and brain, or poor physical coordination; growth deficiencies in both height and weight before and after birth; facial abnormalities, such as short eye slits, droopy eyelids, thin upper lip, and mid-face and jaw deformities; and poorly formed organ systems, including heart, kidney, genital, bone, and joint. In addition, children with FAS can have problems with learning, attention, hyperactivity, memory and problem solving, impulsiveness, speech, and hearing.

There is no way of knowing how much alcohol will cause a birth defect. It appears that *any* drinking increases the risk of birth defects. For that reason, medical experts recommend that pregnant women abstain from alcohol use.

MEDICATION

Whether it is an over-the-counter pain pill or a prescription drug for cardiovascular illness, medication and alcohol can interact in unforeseen and dangerous ways. One estimate is that alcohol and medication combinations may be a factor in 25 percent of all hospital emergency room admissions.

Doctors write 14 billion prescriptions every year, and about 70 percent of the adult population drinks occasionally. So it is likely that at some point, alcohol and medications would be in the bloodstream at the same time. How dangerous is the interaction between alcohol and medication?

Both drugs and alcohol travel through the bloodstream to the organ or tissue where they produce some effect. Gradually they are metabolized out of the system and eliminated from the body. The drugs' ability to reach the organ or tissue and do its work is called its availability. Alcohol can alter the availability of a drug in several ways. A large dose of alcohol may inhibit the body's ability to metabolize the drug because the alcohol is competing with the drug for the same metabolizing enzymes. Enzymes activated by long-term alcoholic consumption may transform some drugs into toxic chemicals.

Alcohol can change the reaction to many medications. Chronic alcohol abuse can require an increased dosage of some anesthetics in order to lose consciousness. When used with alcohol, some antibiotics may cause nausea, headaches, vomiting, and convulsions. Anticoagulants slow down the blood's ability to clot, but alcohol can either enhance or reduce these drugs' abilities. Alcohol increases the sedative effect of some antidepressants, which impairs driving skills. The effectiveness of antidiabetic medications can either be prolonged or decreased with acute alcohol consumption, causing incorrect blood sugar levels. Antipsychotic medications lessen delusions and hallucinations but when used with alcohol can impair coordination, induce fatal breathing difficulties, and cause liver damage.

There are some medicines, like aspirin, that can be taken with alcohol without causing dangerous side effects. However, a person who drinks should always use caution when mixing medicines with alcohol. Most over-the-counter drugs will have a warning label if the combination causes side effects. If the medicine was prescribed by a doctor, both the prescribing doctor and the pharmacist who fills the prescription will know whether the drug can become dangerous when used with alcohol.

In addition to the toll that alcohol abuse takes on a person's mind and body, alcoholism has a high social cost as well.

4

ALCOHOLISM'S EFFECT ON SOCIETY

"**A**lcoholism is like a thief in the night. It can steal up on you and seize your life, liberty and pursuit of happiness before you comprehend what has happened," wrote former U.S. senator George McGovern in his 1996 book *Terry: My Daughter's Life-And-Death Struggle with Alcoholism.*

In the book, McGovern describes the sadness, pain, anger, and guilt of having a daughter who died drunk in a snowdrift at the age of 45. "How could this have happened?" McGovern asked. "My lovable little girl who had given me ten thousand laughs, countless moments of affection and joy, and, yes, years of anxiety and disappointment—now frozen to death like some deserted outcast?"

The straight answer is that Teresa Jane McGovern was an alcoholic—one of 20 million alcoholics in the United States. She died as over 100,000 other American alcoholics do every year. The difference with Terry was that she was the daughter of a prominent family. She had campaigned across the country in 1972 when her father was the Democract Party's candidate for president of the United States. The moment her body was identified, her death was news around the world.

McGovern's memoir reflects the painful loss experienced not only by alcoholics but also by everyone whose life is touched and torn apart by their actions. In the case of Terry McGovern, those lives included her parents, three sisters, a brother, a large circle of friends, and Terry's two young daughters, Marian and Colleen.

In her own journal, Terry recorded a life out of control: "Drive back to Madison after Christmas holidays. Started drinking about two hours away from Madison—was pretty drunk when I got to town, snowing, drove off elevated driveway. Got drunker, screamed at Marian and Colleen out of my own fear about drinking, they were sitting on the couch, both crying."

Another journal entry: "Drunk for Colleen's 4th birthday party. Passed out halfway through, woke up on the bedroom floor."

ALCOHOLISM AND FAMILIES

Experts estimate that 6.6 million children under 18 years of age live in households with at least one alcoholic parent. More than 76 million people have been exposed to alcoholism in the family. Research suggests that these 6.6 million children are at risk for a range of cognitive, emotional, and behavioral problems.

Recent research has indicated there is a link between substance abuse and child maltreatment. A 1996 study by the Children of Alcoholics Foundation found that 40 percent of the reported cases of child abuse, involving 480,000 children, involved the use of alcohol or other drugs. The percentage is even higher in cases of emotional abuse and neglect; alcohol and/or drug use has been linked to over half of these cases, and neglect is the major reason that children are removed from a home in which parents have alcohol or other drug problems.

Neglect may be the reason that children from homes with alcoholic or drug-abusing parents suffer from more mental and emotional problems than other children in the United States. These children often have more physical problems and illnesses as well—possibly as a result of fetal alcohol syndrome—and are more likely to have behavioral problems and conduct disorder. The children lack guidance and positive role models at home, and frequently suffer from depression, anxiety, or low self-esteem. When they grow older, these children are more likely to have problems with alcohol and other drugs themselves.

Another common problem associated with alcohol abuse is domestic violence. This is different from child abuse because it occurs when one member of a relationship, such as a parent, hits or abuses the other parent. In 95 percent of cases, men are responsible for the assaults against their spouse, ex-spouse, or girlfriend.

Because domestic violence is a pattern of behavior, not a one-time occurrence, it is likely that episodes of verbal or physical violence may become more severe. The abuser may eventually broaden his attacks to include the child or children in the family as well. Children may be hit or threatened by the abuser as a way of punishing or controlling the adult victim of domestic violence. They may be unintentionally

Incidences of domestic violence and child abuse are greater in families where one member has a drinking problem.

injured by acts of violence that occur when they are present. And it is very likely that even if the children are not attacked directly, they will experience serious emotional damage as a result of living in a violent household.

In addition, several studies have shown that children from alcoholic families report higher levels of depression, anxiety, and stress. Children from homes with alcoholic parents often demonstrate behavioral problems such as lying, stealing, fighting, truancy, and school behavior problems.

ADULT CHILDREN OF ALCOHOLICS

In 1983, Janet Geringer Woititz wrote *Adult Children Of Alcoholics,* a ground-breaking book that describes life in a family where one or both parents are alcoholics. The book sold two million copies in the United States, Canada, England, Australia, and New Zealand. By 1987, it was on the *New York Times* Best-Seller List and stayed there for 45 weeks.

Woititz describes life as the child of an alcoholic by posing a question: "When is a child not a child? When a child lives with alcoholism. But more correctly, when is a child not childlike? You certainly looked like a child and dressed like a child. Other people saw you as a child, unless they got close enough to that edge of sadness in your eyes or that worried look on your brow."

The child of an alcoholic is robbed of that carefree part of childhood when children are free to focus on whatever interests them at the moment. In homes where one or both parents are alcoholic, children take on adult responsibilities.

"If both your parents were alcoholic, life was even less predictable, except they took turns getting worse," Woititz wrote. "Being home was like being in hell. The tension was so thick that you could cut it with a knife. That nervous, angry feeling was in the air. Nobody had to say a word, as everybody could feel it. It was extremely tense and uncomfortable. Yet there was no way to get away from it, no place to hide and you wondered 'Will it ever end?'"

In the book, Woititz lists the ways that alcoholism affects people who grew up in an alcoholic household. This list illustrates just how profoundly an alcoholic parent affects children:

THE ECONOMIC COSTS OF ALCOHOLISM

In 1992, the most recent year for which data was compiled, the economic cost of alcohol abuse and alcoholism is calculated at $148 billion. Statistics of this magnitude are hard to comprehend, even when broken down into categories.

Nearly 70 percent of the $148 billion is in lost productivity from illness or premature death. The remaining 30 percent is divided into three categories: 12.7 percent is in treatment and medical

1. Adult children of alcoholics guess at what normal behavior is.
2. Adult children of alcoholics have difficulty following a project through from beginning to end.
3. Adult children of alcoholics lie when it would be just as easy to tell the truth.
4. Adult children of alcoholics judge themselves without mercy.
5. Adult children of alcoholics have difficulty having fun.
6. Adult children of alcoholics take themselves very seriously.
7. Adult children of alcoholics have difficulty with intimate relationships.
8. Adult children of alcoholics overreact to changes over which they have no control.
9. Adult children of alcoholics constantly seek approval and affirmation.
10. Adult children of alcoholics usually feel that they are different from other people.
11. Adult children of alcoholics are super responsible or super irresponsible.
12. Adult children of alcoholics are extremely loyal, even if in the face of evidence that the loyalty is undeserved.
13. Adult children of alcoholics are impulsive. They tend to lock themselves into a course of action without giving serious consideration to alternative behaviors or possible consequences. This impulsivity leads to confusion, self-loathing and loss of control over their environment. In addition, they spend an excessive amount of energy cleaning up the mess.

consequences of alcohol consumption; 9.2 percent is in the cost of motor vehicle crashes; and 8.6 percent is in the cost of alcohol-related crime.

As many as 40 percent of industrial-related fatalities and 47 percent of industrial injuries are linked to alcohol consumption and alcoholism, according to the National Council on Alcohol and Drug Dependence. Absenteeism among alcoholic or problem drinkers is 4 to 8 times greater than normal. Alcoholism even affects family members who are not drinkers; nondrinking members of families where someone has an alcohol problem use ten times as much sick leave as members of families in which alcoholism is not present.

ALCOHOL AND AGGRESSION

What part does alcohol play in violent behavior and aggression? A 1980 study found that more than 44 percent of men with alcohol problems admitted to physically abusing their wives, children, and other significant living partners.

Researchers hypothesize that alcohol may encourage aggressive behavior or violence by disrupting normal brain function. Alcohol may weaken brain functions that normally restrain impulsive behaviors, including inappropriate aggression.

But there is also research to show that alcohol may promote aggression because of popular belief. A person who intends to engage in a violent act may drink to bolster his or her courage. The subsequent violence reenforces the popular view of intoxication as a time during which the drinker is not accountable for or subject to the same rules of conduct as a nondrinker.

Social and cultural expectancies may also play a role in the connection between drinking and date rape: the expectation that men are more aggressive when drinking coupled with the expectation that intoxicated women are more sexually receptive and less able to defend themselves.

By impairing the brain's ability to process information, alcohol can lead a person to misjudge social cues and overreact to a threat. Also, the narrowing of attention may lead to an inaccurate assessment of the future risks of carrying out a violent impulse.

WOMEN AND ALCOHOL USE

Fewer women drink alcohol than do men. An estimated 4.6 million women, about a third of the 15.1 million people who abuse or are dependent on alcohol in the United States, are women. However, among the heaviest drinkers, women have more problems than men as a result of their drinking.

Alcohol hits women's bodies harder than men and damages women's livers more than men's. A greater percentage of female drinkers die from suicides, alcohol-related accidents, cirrhosis of the liver, and circulatory

Alcohol appears to be harder on women's bodies than it is on men's. The risks for women who drink include a greater rate of cirrhosis and liver disease, and the possibility of giving birth to a child with fetal alcohol syndrome.

diseases. In addition, women who drink while they are pregnant may give birth to children with fetal alcohol syndrome.

Women's drinking habits tend to mirror those of the people around them. In other words, a woman tends to drink in the same pattern as her husband, siblings, or close friends. The marital status of women appears to modify the effects of genetic influence on drinking habits. Studies show a marriage or marriage-like relationship lessens the effect of an inherited liability for problem drinking. Women who have never married, or are separated or divorced, are more likely to drink heavily and experience alcohol-related problems than women who are married.

Women ages 18 to 34 report higher rates of drinking-related problems than older women. But middle-aged women (age 35 to 49) have a higher incidence of alcoholism. When women experience drinking-related problems, they enter treatment sooner than men.

ALCOHOL AND MINORITIES

In the United States, 68.3 percent of whites, 64.5 percent of Hispanics and 55.6 percent of African Americans use alcohol. Death rates from alcoholism are highest for African Americans, although a higher percent of African Americans than whites abstain from using alcohol. This means that the high rates of medical problems seen in African Americans occur among a smaller percentage of that population when compared to whites.

In a California study, Asians had lower rates of drinking and alcohol abuse than whites, and their alcohol-related mortality was lower than in any other group. Motor vehicle crash rates involving Asians and alcohol were 5.39 per 100,000. This is lower than African Americans (8.02), whites (8.15), and Hispanics (9.16) per 100,000.

Incidence of alcohol abuse varies among the Native American cultures. Alcohol abuse is a factor in the five leading causes of death for Native Americans as a whole, including motor vehicle crashes, alcoholism, cirrhosis, suicide, and homicide. The incidence of vehicle crashes involving Native Americans is 5.5 times higher than the rate among the general population.

COMORBIDITY

Alcoholism is an illness. When two or more illnesses are present in the same person, that condition is called comorbidity. These illnesses can be medical or psychiatric and may occur one at a time or all at the same time.

Alcoholism can increase the severity of psychiatric conditions and

vice versa. Alcoholics are 21 times more likely to have antisocial personality disorder compared with nonalcoholics. This can make diagnosis
and treatment more difficult because patients are forced to choose
among addiction centers, medical clinics, and mental health-related
treatment settings.

Underage drinking is a major problem today; in 1997, according to government statistics, 15 percent of all U.S. eighth graders and 31 percent of high school seniors reported that they had taken more than five drinks at a time on different occasions (this is called "binge" drinking).

5

UNDERAGE DRINKING AND PREVENTION

U nderage drinking is a serious problem in the United States. Alcohol is the most widely used and abused drug among young people. Each year, middle school, junior high, and senior high school students drink 1.1 billion cans of beer and 35 percent of all wine coolers sold in the United States. Even though it is illegal to sell alcohol to someone under the age of 21, about two thirds of teenagers who drink say that they can buy their own alcoholic beverages.

In our society, the pressure to drink alcohol begins early. *The Weekly Reader National Survey on Drugs and Alcohol* reports that 30 percent of children in grades four through six said they had received "a lot" of pressure from their classmates to drink beer. The same survey said that 56 percent of students in grades 5 to 12 say that alcohol advertising encourages them to drink. People 13 to 15 years old are at high risk to begin drinking. First use of alcohol typically begins around the age of 13.

About 9.5 million Americans between the ages of 12 and 20 have at least one drink each month. Of that group, 4.4 million are considered binge drinkers. Binge drinkers are defined as those who drink five or more drinks in a row on a single occasion. Binge drinking often begins around age 13 and tends to increase during adolescence. It peaks in young adulthood in people ages 18–22 and then begins to decrease for most people by their early thirties. In a 1994 survey, 28 percent of high school seniors and 41 percent of 21- to 22-year-olds participated in binge drinking.

Heavy drinkers—those who drink five or more drinks on the same occasion for five days a month—account for 1.9 million of those 9.5 million underage drinkers.

Not too surprisingly, the use of alcohol or other drugs at an early age is an indicator of future alcohol or drug problems. In a study of 43,000 interviews

Some young adults may turn to alcohol to escape from feelings of stress or frustration.

done by the National Institute on Alcohol Abuse and Alcoholism, the younger the age at which a person begins drinking alcohol, the greater the chance that the person will develop an alcohol-related disorder.

Of those who began drinking before the age of 15, 40 percent were classified with alcohol dependence at some time in their lives. Of those who begin drinking alcohol at age 17, 24.5 percent become alcohol dependent. Those people who wait until ages 21 and 22 to begin drinking alcohol account for only 10 percent of those who become alcohol dependent. Researchers estimate that for every year a young person does not begin drinking, his or her risk of alcohol dependence decreases by 14 percent.

In 1997 the U.S. Secretary of Health and Human Services, Donna E. Shalala, said this study added new evidence about the need to see underage drinking as a serious problem. "Parents, schools, and communities need to say to our young people with one voice that underage drinking can jeopardize health and lifetime prospects," she said.

WHY DO YOUNG ADULTS DRINK?

There are various theories on why underage people drink. Some say that adolescence is a time when kids "try out" adult social roles. Others believe that early use of alcohol is a symptom of a broader range of social problems. Adolescents who drink may have problems not only with alcohol, but also with school, illegal drugs, delinquent behavior, and family life.

Richard Heyman, chairman of the American Academy of Pediatrics Committee on Substance Abuse, said he believes teenagers abuse alcohol for a variety of reasons. "Some kids start because they're a little rebellious," Heyman said. "Others start because they're offered alcoholic beverages by a friend or an adult. And some drink because it is portrayed as absolutely normal by the media, by advertising agencies and by the sports industry."

Heyman said kids who are chronically depressed or have been abused use alcohol and drugs to make themselves feel better. He said that some kids begin to use alcohol because they have an "image gap."

"The bigger the gap between how a teenager sees himself and how he wishes he looks, acts, or seems, the more likely he is to need something to fill that gap," Heyman stated. "A lot of kids choose alcohol and drugs to do that."

He also noted that there are differences between teen and adult drinking patterns: "Adults who use beer responsibly use it to quench their thirst and to feel good. But kids who drink beer don't drink it to quench their thirst or to feel good. They drink it to get smashed. Unlike most adults, kids drink to get drunk."

AGE DOES MAKE A DIFFERENCE

Researchers at Duke University Medical Center and the Durham Veterans Administration Medical Center in North Carolina are convinced that alcohol has different effects on drinkers according to their age. These researchers studied the effects of alcohol on young adults ranging in age from 21 to 30 and found that a low dosage of alcohol— one drink—impaired learning and memory in the younger adults more than the older adults.

MIXED MESSAGES
AND THE MEDIA

In the United States, alcohol is often glorified and rarely denigrated. Alcohol is glamorized by rock stars and advertised during the Super Bowl. It is estimated that children in the United States will see alcohol consumed on TV, in movies, and through personal observation an average of 75,000 times before they reach the legal drinking age.

The National Council on Alcoholism and Drug Dependence lists these statistics about the influence of alcohol beverage advertising:

- A survey of children aged 9 to 11 demonstrated high rates of recognition and recall of both the brand name and product associated with television commercials featuring the Budweiser frogs, even when compared to commercials that appeal to kids and characters from children's programming, including Tony the Tiger, Smokey the Bear, and the Power Rangers.

- In grades 5 to 12, 56 percent of students say that alcohol advertising encourages them to drink.

- Watching beer commercials on TV increases the expectations of children that they will be beer-drinkers as adults.

Alcohol advertisements overwhelmingly associate drinking with positively valued activities and consequences such as romance, sociability, and relaxation and create a climate in which drinking is presented as normal, appropriate, and benevolent. More subtly, the use of alcohol is linked to happiness, wealth, power, prestige, sophistication, success, maturity, athletic ability, virility, romance, creativity, sexual satisfaction, and other positive images. Adolescents who are heavily exposed to advertising were more likely to agree that drinkers possess valued characteristics such as being attractive, athletic, or successful.

Lead investigator Scott Swartzwelder said that the scientific evidence proves that even occasional and moderate drinking could impair a young adult's memory systems much more than that of an adult several years older. When subjects were given two drinks, the results were consistent: the younger the age, the worse the test subjects performed on the memory tests. "If alcohol's effects varied that much within such a narrow age range, then there's a compelling reason to believe its effects are even stronger in adolescents and children," Swartzwelder said.

There is also evidence of physical damage that is related to underage drinking. In laboratory studies using animals, high doses of alcohol were found to delay puberty in both female and male test subjects. In addition, large quantities of alcohol given to young rats resulted in slower bone growth and weaker bones. How much of this research applies to young people is not clear, because scientists cannot do such studies on human beings, but as Chapter 3 discussed, the damage alcohol wreaks on the human body is well known and documented.

SOCIAL PROBLEMS

The teenage years are difficult for most young people because social development is such a complex process. It can be difficult for an adolescent to gain self-confidence, maintain friendships, and succeed in school and outside activities. Awkwardness, confusion, hurt, and anger are common feelings of growing up.

When alcohol is used to numb those feelings, the alcohol becomes a substitute for learning how to deal with those feelings. Social development is slowed down or even stopped. The person becomes dependent on the alcohol to relieve those feelings, and the addiction of alcohol is added to the problems of social development. When the pressure becomes too much, some students decide that suicide is the only way to resolve their problems. In 50 to 60 percent of adolescent suicides, use of alcohol is involved.

Alcohol abuse also has a significant effect on academic performance. Among college students there is a clear connection between alcohol use and grades. Students with D or F grade-point averages drink three times as much as those who earn As. And a 1998 survey of 4,390 high school seniors and dropouts reported that within the preceding year, 80 percent said they had either gotten drunk, gone on drinking binges, or drove after drinking. More than half of this group admitted that drinking had caused them to miss school or work, get arrested, feel sick, or have a car crash.

DRINKING AND DRIVING

Although young people are less likely to drive than adults, their crash rates are substantially higher than the accident rates of adult drivers. Half of all car accidents—the leading cause of death among teenagers—involve alcohol. For people aged 15 to 34, car accidents are the single largest cause of death. In fact, youth is cited as one of the most important variables in car accidents. This is because young drivers are inexperienced at both driving and drinking.

In 1994, almost 7,800 persons ages 16 to 20 were drivers in fatal car accidents. Although it is illegal for anyone that age to drink, 23 percent of those drivers had registered blood alcohol concentrations (BACs) in their blood of 0.01 percent or higher. Researchers estimate that with each 0.02 percent increase in BAC levels above 0.00, the 16- to 20-year-old driver is at greater risk for a crash than older drivers.

The good news is that young drivers seem to be getting the message that drinking and driving is dangerous. According to statistics published by Mothers Against Drunk Driving (MADD), the number of fatal crashes involving intoxicated young adult drivers dropped by 14.3 percent from 1983 to 1994. This represents the largest decrease of any age group during this time period.

ALCOHOL AND TEEN SEXUALITY

The expectancy that alcohol makes a male more virile and a female more sexually attractive also increases the risk that alcohol will be involved in either risky sexual activity or criminal sexual activity, especially by young adults.

Among sexually active teens, those who average five or more drinks daily were nearly three times less likely to use condoms, placing them at greater risk for HIV infection, other sexually transmitted diseases, and pregnancy. Of all teens who drink, 16 percent use condoms less often after drinking.

Researchers estimate that alcohol use is implicated in one to two

A police officer tests the blood-alcohol content of these two young men using an electronic device called a breathalyzer. Drinking and driving is one of the leading causes of death among teenagers in the United States.

thirds of sexual assault and acquaintance or date rape cases among teens and college students. A survey of high school students found that 18 percent of females and 39 percent of males think it is acceptable for a boy to force sex if the girl is stoned or drunk.

THE WARNING SIGNS

Parents who think their son or daughter may have a drinking problem should look for the warning signs that their teenage child is abusing alcohol. Physical signs include increased health complaints, confusion in thought process or ideas, frequent and long-lasting fatigue, and disturbed sleeping and eating patterns. Psychological and emotional signs may include withdrawal from parents and other family members, increases in unprovoked hostility and uncooperativeness, lack of interest in communication, increased depression, mood swings, increase in irresponsible behavior, and heightened levels of irritability.

Social and interpersonal signs include changes in friends or peer group toward a more deviant social group, the adoption of new styles of dress or musical interests, and encounters with legal authorities. School warning signs include a drop in grades, unexcused absences and tardy incidents, and increases in discipline problems.

Of course, some of the warning signs of alcohol abuse could be symptomatic of other problems. For example, a disturbance in eating and sleeping patterns may be the result of conflict within the family, the break-up of a romantic relationship, or school anxiety. Extreme fatigue may be a sign of a medical condition or psychiatric disorder.

If parents do feel their son or daughter has a drinking problem, they should confront the child and attempt to steer him or her toward counseling. A *USA Today Magazine* article offered the following suggestions for parents who suspect that their teen is an alcoholic:

- Do not regard this as a family disgrace.

- Do not nag, preach, or lecture the child. Chances are the teenager already has told himself or herself everything the parent may be trying to say.

- Avoid making threats—no longer allowing the child to live at home if he or she continues to abuse alcohol, for example— unless you think them through carefully and definitely intend to carry them out.

Organizations such as Mothers Against Drunk Driving, founded in 1980, have worked to raise young adults' awareness of the danger of alcohol and drug abuse.

- Do not do for alcoholics what they must do for themselves. While the teen should be guided away from alcohol, becoming sober is a decision he or she will have to make.
- Offer love, support, and understanding.

PREVENTION OF TEEN ALCOHOL ABUSE

Advertising to counter the influence of ads for alcoholic beverages is finding increased support as a means to prevent drinking by adolescents or teenagers. An article in the 1994 issue of the *American Journal of Public Health* indicates that counter-advertising to prevent or delay

DO YOU HAVE A DRINKING PROBLEM?

Teenagers who believe they have a drinking problem can take the following quiz developed by Alcoholics Anonymous:

1. Do you drink because you have problems? To relax?

2. Do you drink when you get mad at other people, your friends, or parents?

3. Do you prefer to drink alone, rather than with others?

4. Are your grades starting to slip? Are you goofing off on your job?

5. Did you every try to stop drinking or drink less—and fail?

6. Have you begun to drink in the morning, before school or work?

7. Do you gulp your drinks?

8. Do you ever had loss of memory due to your drinking?

9. Do you lie about your drinking?

10. Do you ever get into trouble when you're drinking?

11. Do you get drunk when you drink, even when you don't mean to?

12. Do you think it's cool to be able to hold your liquor?

More than two "yes" answers could indicate a drinking problem.

drinking among young people "represents a reasonable strategy. To be effective, it must compete with commercial alcoholic advertisements in terms of quality, interest and frequency of exposure. Equal time requirements or the dedication of alcohol tax funds for the production and airing of health messages may be necessary to achieve these goals." Proposed funding sources for counter advertising include a "dime a drink" tax increase on alcohol that would generate nearly $4 billion in new revenue the first year and $23 billion over five years.

Current public service advertising and industry-sponsored "moderation messages" are considered inadequate by prevention advocates. For example, in 1990, Anheuser Busch spent only three percent of its $459 million advertising budget on its "Know When to Say When" advertising campaign supporting moderate drinking. Prevention advocates argue that public service announcements are too infrequent to have much effect. And since the deregulation of the broadcast industry in the 1980s, fewer public service announcements have been shown.

A young child sits quietly, waiting for her alcoholic parent to wake up. Tragically, there is evidence that indicates alcoholism can be passed genetically from parents to children.

6

·A NEW CATEGORY
OF DISEASE

U ntil the last few decades, the mainstream medical establishment dis-
dained the study of substance abuse as a disease. Alcoholics or drug
addicts were considered losers, people who just couldn't control their
behavior, couldn't face reality, or were afraid of their emotions or of responsibility. Although even today there is not universal agreement on this point,
many health care professionals have come to believe that addiction to alcohol
is a disease.

Mark S. Gold, M.D., author of *The Good News About Drugs and Alcohol,*
said the concept that addiction is a disease is one of the most important
medical discoveries of the 20th century "because it has helped millions of
people to stop blaming themselves for their illness." Gold defines addiction
to alcohol or any drug this way: "Addiction is a disease characterized by
repetitive and destructive use of one or more mood-altering substances, and
stems from a biological vulnerability exposed or induced by environmental
forces."

Genetic studies indicate that alcoholism tends to run in families and,
therefore, that a biological (or genetic) vulnerability exists for alcoholism.
Any disorder that can be passed from one generation to the next has a biological basis, called inheritability. In studies of adopted children, the children
of alcoholic parents who were adopted in infancy and raised by nonalcoholic
parents were still more likely to be alcoholic than adopted children of nonalcoholics who were raised in families where one or both parents had a problem with alcohol.

Evidence exists that brain function is different in the children of alcoholics.
In animal studies, rats and mice have been selectively bred according to their
preference or nonpreference for alcohol. Rats that preferred alcohol (P rats)
and rats that did not prefer alcohol (NP rats) were both given low amounts of

alcohol. The NP rats were sedated by the alcohol, but the P rats were stimulated by the alcohol. The researchers found neurochemical differences between the rats, even in P and NP rats that were never given alcohol. They have found similar results in human studies. In addition to these nervous system differences, addicts' bodies are different. Researchers have discovered that the physical responses to alcohol are different in the children of addicts and nonaddicts. A study measuring brain activity found that sons of alcoholics are more sensitive to moderate doses of alcohol than are the general public.

A NEW CATEGORY OF DISEASE

The idea that alcoholism, or substance abuse, is a disease is controversial because of the way that it presents itself. Many people see alcoholism not as a disease, but as a problem that could be avoided if only the person had enough willpower to stop drinking. Because drinking is pleasurable, its negative side occurs by choice, they argue.

In his book *Alcoholism: The Facts,* Dr. Goodwin explains the controversy over alcoholism as a disease this way:

> Is lead poisoning a disease? Lead poisoning is diagnosed by a specific set of symptoms: abdominal pain, headache, convulsions, coma. Alcoholism also is diagnosed by specific symptoms. Both lead poisoning and alcoholism are "medical" problems, meaning, that doctors are supposed to know something about them and possibly be of help.

> One reason people, including doctors, have trouble viewing alcoholism as a disease like cancer is that alcoholism is associated with having fun, and fun is not usually associated with disease. (Where does that leave syphilis? Is sex less fun than drinking?)

> The point is this: why or how a person "catches" a disease is not relevant. If some "self-indulgent" people enjoyed lead and ate it like popcorn, this would not change the diagnosis of lead intoxication. Diseases are known by their manifestations as well as their causes, and why alcoholics drink is irrelevant to the diagnosis of alcoholism.

Enoch Gordis, M.D., director of the National Institute of Alcohol Abuse and Alcoholism, believes that some people's reluctance to see alcoholism as a disease is due to the fact that modern treatment of

In a scientific study, rats were bred with or without a preference for alcohol, and the differences in their reaction to the drug was tested. The researchers found differences in the brains and neurological systems of the two different types of rats, even when neither type was given alcohol.

alcoholism began with Alcoholics Anonymous, which was created outside the mainstream of medicine.

"Some people ask: how can we say that alcoholism is a disease, when most treatment is talking and the patient recovers by using willpower? Don't these facts prove that failure to recover is misconduct or a character defect?" said Gordis. "The answer is not that alcoholism is a sin or character defect, but that we are dealing with a new category of disease."

Gordis points out that, throughout the history of medicine, the concept of disease has changed. With alcoholism and other addictions, that concept is once again expanded.

Gordis explains that in the brain, there are neurons (he calls them "reward circuits") that provide good feelings in response to behavior that sustains life: the normal drives for food, shelter, and love. When these are joined by a drive for alcohol or illegal drugs, a substance that is destructive to the body, the need for the drug overrides the reward circuits. The substance that is being abused becomes more important than anything else. "What has gone wrong in the alcoholic," Gordis commented, "is the development of a pathological [meaning caused by disease] motivational drive state."

GENETIC, OR DECISION?

After 25 years of studies using twins and adopted children, it has been clearly demonstrated that a certain part of becoming an alcoholic is genetic. Researchers are now looking for the specific genes that put a person at risk for alcoholism. Once researchers learn how these genes work, they will be able to understand how to create effective treatments.

The issue of the genetic basis for alcoholism raises interesting questions in the legal profession. When someone commits a crime under the influence of alcohol, the law does not recognize alcoholism as a defense or an excuse. But what happens in the years ahead, when neuroscience and genetics offer new explanations for the biological origins of alcoholism as a disease? When is it acceptable to blame the disease of alcoholism for a person's actions, and when must the fact that the person chose to drink be blamed?

No one begins drinking with the intention of becoming an alcoholic and destroying his life and the lives of those around him. But every person has the choice of whether or not to begin drinking. So when is an individual responsible for his or her alcoholism?

"A child of an alcoholic parent is at high risk and is obligated to monitor carefully any increase in his drinking while drinking is still under normal cognitive control," Gordis says. "Young people who are

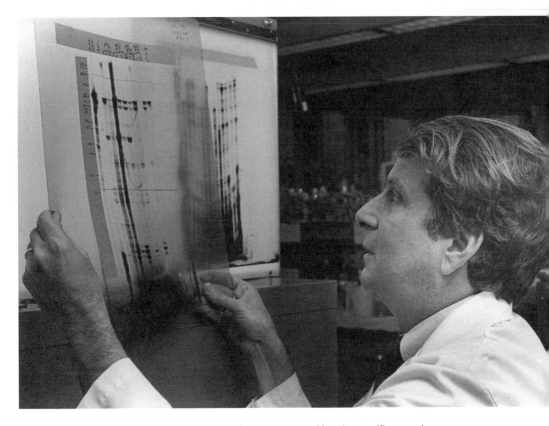

A doctor examines a DNA chart. Researchers are now seeking the specific gene that puts a person at a higher risk for alcoholism.

less sensitive than their friends to the effects of alcohol are likely to escalate their drinking and are at greatly increased risk for alcoholism as adults.

"In the case of an alcoholic person, when [he or she] becomes sober and understands the troubles [that] drinking has caused . . . [he or she] is responsible for making every effort to remain abstinent."

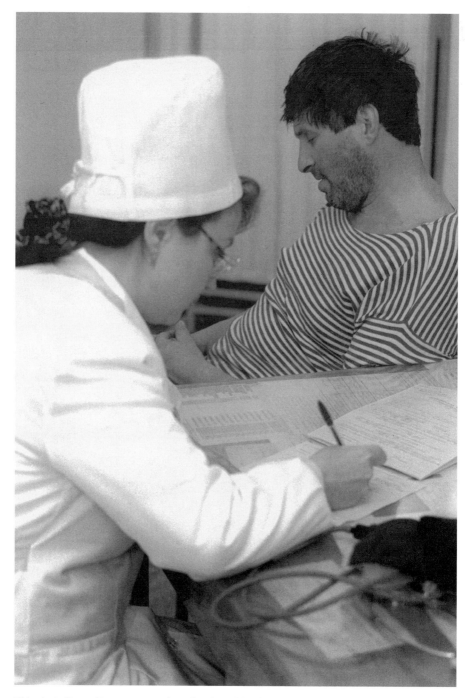

This alcoholic, seeking treatment, is registering with a local clinic. Ending dependence on alcohol can be very difficult, both physically and psychologically.

7

TREATMENT OF ALCOHOLISM

The ability to stop drinking alcohol permanently is a goal that is difficult for alcoholics. Because alcohol is both physically and mentally addictive, alcoholics who stop drinking are dealing with medical and psychological symptoms that are traumatic and recurring.

When people recover from alcoholism, their stories often have a spiritual aspect to them, no matter what that person's religious affiliation might be. A belief in "a Power greater" than the individual is the basis of the most popular treatment of alcoholism in the United States: Alcoholics Anonymous (AA). Today, AA has nearly 2 million members worldwide. In the United States, more than 50,000 AA groups meet on a regular basis.

Early in the development of AA, the group developed a suggested program for recovery called The Twelve Steps of Alcoholics Anonymous:

1. We admitted we were powerless over alcohol—that our lives had become unmanageable.

2. Came to believe that a Power greater than ourselves could restore us to sanity.

3. Made a decision to turn our will and our lives over to the care of God as we understood Him.

4. Make a searching and fearless moral inventory of ourselves.

5. Admitted to God, to ourselves and to another human being the exact nature of our wrongs.

6. Were entirely ready to have God remove all these defects of character.

7. Humbly asked Him to remove our shortcomings.

8. Made a list of all persons we had harmed, and became willing to make amends to them all.

9. Made direct amends to such people wherever possible, except when to do so would injure them or others.

10. Continued to take personal inventory and when we were wrong promptly admitted it.

11. Sought through prayer and meditation to improve our conscious contact with God as we understood Him, praying only for knowledge of His will for us and the power to carry that out.

12. Having had a spiritual awakening as the result of these steps, we tried to carry this message to alcoholics and to practice these principles in all our affairs.

The Twelve Steps of AA do not specifically mention the disease of alcoholism. Yet the Twelve Steps list includes this addendum: "It will be pointed out that all available medical testimony indicates that alcoholism is a progressive illness, that it can not be cured in the ordinary sense of the term, but that it can be arrested through total abstinence from alcohol in any form."

Alcoholics Anonymous has been called a religion by some observers. Doctor Donald Goodwin, author of *Alcoholism: The Facts*, explains the religious nature of AA this way:

> To the extent that it is a "religion," AA is one of the least doctrinaire and authoritarian religions imaginable. Atheists can belong to AA as comfortably as believers. There is no formal doctrine and no insistence that anyone accept a particular explanation for alcoholism. AA gives drinkers something to do when they are not drinking. It offers occasions for the soul-satisfying experience of helping someone else. It provides companions who do not drink. And it provides hope for those who need it desperately—the alcoholic and his family—and instant help for the man who wants to get back on the wagon and can't quite make it.

FAMILY SUPPORT GROUPS

As alcoholics in AA began to recover from their illness, families of alcoholics began to express a need for a group that could provide understanding and support. They saw how using the same philosophy could improve family relationships that were still a problem even after the alcoholic became sober.

A family meets with an alcohol counselor. Family counseling and therapy are important components of treatment for alcoholism.

Family groups started meeting as early as 1935, the first year AA was founded. By the early 1950s, AA co-founder Bill Wilson suggested to his wife, Lois, that she open an office to provide support for families of alcoholics. They adopted the same Twelve Steps philosophy, and the organization became Al-Anon Family Groups.

In the mid-1950s, the problems of children of alcoholics began to be formally recognized. In 1957, the teenage son of AA and Al-Anon parents started Alateen for teenagers.

Today Al-Anon has a worldwide membership of 600,000, serving more than 33,000 groups in 112 countries. This includes more than 4,000 Alateen groups. What began as a "coffee and cake" group for the wives of AA members is now an organization that includes men, parents, Al-Anon members also recovering in AA, adult children, gays/lesbians, brothers/sisters, divorced men and women, widows and widowers.

Alateen groups have expanded to include preteen family members.

OTHER TREATMENTS

Although the dominant form of therapy in the United States is support groups like Alcoholics Anonymous, there are other treatments for alcoholism. Drugs, psychotherapy, behavior therapy, and cognitive therapy are all accepted methods of treatment.

When alcoholism was considered a character defect, the misery of alcohol withdrawal was seen as a harsh, but justifiable, consequence of excessive drinking. However, today doctors know that without medication, repeated withdrawals can cause permanent brain damage. Drug derivatives of benzodiazepine, such as Librium, Valium, Serx, and Ativan, can be used to help ease a person through alcohol withdrawal. The benzodiazepines drugs calm the problems that the central nervous system experiences after alcohol withdrawal.

There are several other types of drugs prescribed for alcohol addiction. These drugs work by treating the various symptoms of being dependent on or withdrawing from alcohol. Antidepressant medications, such as Prozac, enhance the neurotransmitter serotonin's calming effect on brain cells and reduce drinking in both animals and human. The drug lithium, commonly used to reduce symptoms of bipolar disorder (manic depression), has also been used to treat alcoholism. Although

Former First Lady Betty Ford speaks during a group discussion on alcohol and drug abuse. In the 1970s Ford developed an alcohol problem; since becoming sober, she has been an advocate of treatment for alcoholism and helped found the Betty Ford Clinic to help people recover from substance-abuse problems.

these drugs help relieve feelings of anxiety and depression, they do not necessarily deter alcoholics from using alcohol.

A commonly prescribed drug that deters alcoholics from drinking is called Antabuse. This drug makes the person who takes it physically ill when he or she drinks alcohol. However, the drug is only effective when recovering alcoholics are diligent about taking it. Alcoholics report that they intentionally "forget" to take the drug when the urge to drink again becomes overwhelming.

Some therapists use Antabuse in a more restricted way. In order to attain sobriety for his or her patient for one month, the therapist "takes over" the responsibility for their patient's drinking and dispenses the drug every three to four days. The alcoholic agrees to take the drug under the supervision of the therapist, thereby eliminating the possibility that alcohol will enter his or her system.

After a month of sobriety, the therapist and alcoholic "renegotiate" their contract for another month. Ideally, this leads to six months of sobriety. Why six months? There is evidence that most relapses occur within the first six months after quitting alcohol.

In *Alcoholism: The Facts*, Doctor Goodwin, who treats patients with Antabuse, writes that this drug should be used more in the United States: "Supervised Antabuse is a much neglected treatment. . . . It should be tried elsewhere. It often seems to work."

PSYCHOTHERAPY

The treatment of alcoholism through AA and drug therapies does not concentrate on trying to understand how or why a person becomes an alcoholic. Psychotherapy attempts to do this through understanding the origins of the problem.

Sigmund Freud, the founder of psychoanalysis, believed that a person's psychosexual development was made up of four stages. The first of these is the "oral," stage; Freud believed that the infant receives gratification from placing objects in his or her mouth. Because drinking is an oral activity, Freud believed that alcoholism is the result of an oral conflict early in childhood. Psychotherapy can be used to help the alcoholic understand and overcome his childhood-related conflict.

Another form of psychotherapy used to treat alcoholism is transactional analysis. The philosophy is that each person has a child, an adult, and a parent in his or her mental makeup, and that these forces are constantly interacting. The "parent" figure of the subconscious includes the rules and guidelines that society and the person's upbringing provide. The person may turn to alcohol to reduce stress or guilt over perceived infractions of these rules. Transactional analysis helps the alcoholic to find less destructive ways to react to outside stress. This is often accomplished in a group therapy situation.

Another type of therapy physically conditions alcoholics to dislike alcohol. Alcoholics taste or smell alcohol just before a pre-administered drug makes them nauseated. Or they receive electric shocks, take a drug that induces panic, or imagine unpleasant effects of drinking. This is called behavior therapy.

Operant conditioning is the system of rewarding people when they achieve desired behavior and punishing them when they do not. The goal is for alcoholics to continue the desired behavior after the rewards and punishments have stopped. Operant conditioning can be anything from patients in a hospital setting receiving tokens for appropriate behavior to a personal reward system set up by the individual.

The theory behind another type of psychotherapy, called cognitive therapy, is that a person can change behavior by changing his or her thoughts. Replacing negative thoughts with positive thoughts eventually helps alcoholics think better of themselves. One form of cognitive therapy is relapse prevention. With this method, alcoholics identify the situations where they are at high risk for relapsing. Then they develop coping skills for either avoiding those situations or finding new ways to act in those situations.

RELAPSE

"It is the great mystery of addictions," writes Donald Goodwin in *Alcoholism: The Facts.* "Why, after months or years of abstinence, does the smoker smoke again, the junkie shoot up again, the alcoholic fall off the wagon?" There is evidence that about 90 percent of alcoholics are likely to experience at least one relapse over the four-year period following abstinence.

It is difficult for the nonalcoholic to understand why anyone would give up his or her hard-won sobriety to fall back into the misery of alcohol dependence. When an alcoholic relapses, the person's family members are left feeling angry and hopeless. And sometimes the professionals trying to help them recover share those feelings.

"Both the doctor and the patient should be prepared for relapses," says Goodwin. "Alcoholism, by definition, is a chronic relapsing

One of the hardest things for a recovering alcoholic to do is to stay sober. Relapses are common; one study says approximately 90 percent of alcoholics attempting to quit experience at least one relapse during their first four years of sobriety.

condition, although relapses are not inevitable. It resembles manic-depressive disease in this regard and also has similarities to such chronic medical illnesses as diabetes and multiple sclerosis."

Goodwin says that relapse can be partly explained by a concept called stimulus generalization. This means that certain things remind a person of other things. In the case of alcohol, a time of day may remind the recovering alcoholic of happy hour at the local pub.

"Every drinker has his own reminders, but there are common themes," Goodwin explains. "Food, sex, holidays, football games, fishing, travel; all have nothing intrinsically to do with drinking but all commonly become associated with drinking and are powerful reminders. Physical feelings become reminders: hunger, fatigue. Moods become reminders: nostalgia, sadness, elation. Anything, in short, can be a reminder and remain a reminder long after a person has stopped drinking."

Research has also shown that the severity of alcohol dependence is a key factor in relapse. Another determinant for relapse is the extent to which the alcoholic's ability to control his actions has been damaged or impaired.

PREDICTING THE FUTURE OF ALCOHOLISM RESEARCH

In 1995, on the 25th anniversary of the founding of the National Institute on Alcohol Abuse and Alcoholism, NIAAA director Enoch Gordis discussed the future of alcoholism research. He predicted that research will uncover two kinds of genes related to alcoholism. In addition to genes that are unique to the alcoholic population, there will be what he called "surprising genes."

"It happens in other fields where you find a gene that is a cognate of something in a worm or a lobster, and you don't know what it is doing in man," Gordis said. By learning the precise role that genes play in causing alcoholism, scientists will also be able to understand more precisely what role environment plays in alcoholism.

As the neurosciences become more advanced, Gordis said he expects researchers to find out more about the intermediate level between how individual cells react and the end behavioral result of those reactions. "I believe that we will be able to relate cognition and emotion to the process of addiction in increasingly more sophisticated ways," Gordis noted.

The imaging technology of today that allows scientists to watch how alcohol's toxicity affects the brain will be expanded. Researchers will be able to use the physical imaging techniques to be able to actually see the chemical actions of alcoholic craving—the intense need of an alcoholic to drink again, even when the consequences of a relapse are obvious. Some researchers believe craving comes from the generalized stimulus between drinking behavior and environmental cues. Other researchers say craving is a physical appetite urge that varies in intensity and is characterized by withdrawal-like symptoms. These symptoms come from internal as well as external cues. Craving symptoms remind the drinker of both the euphoria of alcohol and the need to avoid the misery of withdrawal.

GOALS OF FUTURE RESEARCH

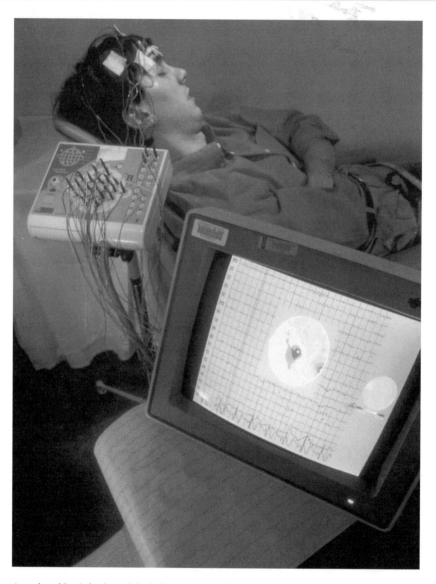

A study subject's brain activity being measured by a researcher. In the future, scientists will continue to search for a cure for alcoholism.

The NIAAA has made it a priority to focus future research efforts in the following areas:

1. Determining which aspects of the vulnerability to alcoholism are inherited. Linking specific traits with specific genes or groups of genes may support innovative ways to interfere with the development of alcoholism.

2. Determining how genetic and nongenetic factors interact in the development of alcoholism. The ability of some nerve cells to undergo long-term adaptive changes in response to environmental stimuli suggests that nature and nurture cannot be considered separately in the development of alcoholism.

3. Increasing efforts to address the special treatment needs of traditionally underserved populations. For example, NIAAA supports the largest and most intensive study of women's drinking habits over time ever conducted in the United States as well as research to develop effective treatments aimed at ethnic and racial minorities, older individuals, and youth.

4. Developing new treatment methods. For example, the NIAAA researchers are searching for medications that act to impede the progression of alcoholism and lessen the risk of relapse in recovering alcoholics. In the near future, this research may be aided by computer-assisted molecular technology for predicting the therapeutic effects of potential medications

5. Another goal of future research is to remove the stigma associated with alcoholism as it provides hope for the millions of people affected by this disease, their families, and society.

Source: National Institute on Alcohol Abuse and Alcoholism

In the area of toxicology, Gordis believes researchers will learn how to prevent or reverse some of alcohol's toxic effects. Future research may be able to answer why some people drink without damaging their liver or brains.

In the field of alcoholic treatment, Gordis said that he believes there will continue to be new medications developed and targeted for certain segments of the alcoholic population. He also believes that there will be a deeper understanding of the way that medication and verbal therapy work together.

Gordis stated that he believes that in the future there will be an increasing respect for science in the formulation of social policy. Scientific research will become more influential in the discussion and enactment of local and national policy on crime, taxation, addiction, and legal standards.

Another area of advancement in the future will be in epidemiology. Epidemiology is the study of alcoholism as a diagnosable disease. The primary aim of alcohol epidemiology is to identify and explain the factors that shape the distribution of alcohol use, abuse, and dependence and consequences in various populations. It is necessary to describe the nature and magnitude of alcohol's impact on individuals and society in order to develop effective prevention, intervention, and treatment. In the future, epidemiology will probably be advanced through insights gained in genetic research and more understanding of the basic science in the alcoholism population.

FINDING A CURE

Although a cure for alcoholism is not yet a reality, Gordis believes that a complete cure is the ultimate goal of alcoholism research.

"How do we reconcile the rally cry 'let's cure alcoholism in our lifetime' with the need to teach about the concept of chronic relapsing illness?" Gordis asked. "Easily. After all, with diabetes, we have a chronic, relapsing disorder, and with arthritis we have the same. In both cases there are treatments that help but no cure. Yet each of the constituency groups for these disease disorders focuses not only on finding better treatments . . . but on the long-term need for a cure."

■　　　　■　　　　■

As the common perception of alcoholism has changed, the treatment of this disease and its related problems has been modified. In the last 25 years, the study and treatment of alcoholism has become an important area of mainstream medical research. Major discoveries have been made in neuroscience and genetics which are creating new treatments for alcoholics, and clinical trials are being used to test new treatments and to examine previously untested, yet traditional, treatment methods.

In the future, treatment of alcoholism will probably combine several of the methods listed in this chapter, while also incorporating a genetic treatment that interferes with a person's specific genes that are related to alcoholism. Treatments will also be specifically developed to help differ-ent segments of the population—young adults, different ethnic groups, and even men and women. Another goal of future research is to remove the stigma associated with alcoholism, as new treatment methods pro-vide hope for the millions of people affected, either directly or indirectly, by this disease.

APPENDIX

FOR MORE INFORMATION

Alcoholics Anonymous (AA) World Services
475 Riverside Drive, 11th Floor
New York, NY 10115
(212) 870-3400
Internet address: http://www.
alcohlics-anonymous.org

Al-Anon Family Group Headquarters
1600 Corporate Landing Parkway
Virginia Beach, VA 23454-5617
Internet address: http://www.
al-anon.alateen.org

For locations of **Al-Anon** or **Alateen**
meetings worldwide, call toll-free,
24 hours a day, 7 days a week:
U.S. (800) 344-2666
Canada (800) 443-4525

American Society of Addiction Medicine
4601 North Park Avenue
Arcade Suite 101
Chevy Chase, MD 20815
(301)656-3920
Internet address: www.asam.org

Mothers Against Drunk Driving (MADD)
P.O. Box 541688
Dallas, TX 75354-1688
Internet address: http://www.madd.org

**National Association of Alcoholism and
Drug Abuse Counselors**
1911 North Fort Myer Drive, Suite 900
Arlington, VA 22209
(703) 741-7686
(800) 548-0497
Internet address: www.naadac.org

**National Association of State Alcohol and
Drug Abuse Directors**
808 17th St. N.W., Suite 410
Washington, D.C. 20001
(202) 293-0090
Internet address: www.nasadad.org

**National Council on Alcoholism and Drug
Dependence (NCADD)**
12 West 21st St.
New York, NY 10010
(800) NCA-CALL
Internet address: http://www.ncadd.org

**National Institute on Alcohol Abuse and
Alcoholism (NIAAA)**
Scientific Communications Branch
6000 Executive Boulevard, Suite 409
Bethesda, MD 20892-7003
(301) 443-3860
Internet address: http://www.niaaa.nih.gov

APPENDIX

SOURCES CITED

Berry, Ralph E. Jr., and James P. Boland. *The Economic Cost of Alcohol Abuse.* New York: The Free Press, 1997.

Gold, Mark. *The Good News About Drugs and Alcohol.* New York: Villard, 1991.

Goodwin, Donald W. *Alcoholism: The Facts.* New York: Oxford University Press, 1997.

Jaffe, Jerome H., ed. *Encyclopedia of Drugs and Alcohol.* New York: MacMillan Library Reference, 1995.

Kinney, Jean. *Clinical Manual of Substance Abuse.* St. Louis: Mosby-Year Book, Inc., 1991.

Lender, Mark Edward, and James Kirby Martin. *Drinking in America.* New York: Macmillan, 1982.

McGovern, George. *Terry: My Daughter's Life-and-Death Struggle with Alcoholism.* New York: Villard, 1996.

National Institute on Alcohol Abuse and Alcoholism. "Alcohol Alert 4: Alcohol and Cognition." (pamphlet). Rockville, Md.: National Institutes of Health, 1989.

———. "Alcohol Alert 5: Alcohol Withdrawal Syndrome." (pamphlet). Rockville, Md.: National Institutes of Health, 1989.

———. "Alcohol Alert 6: Relapse and Craving." (pamphlet). Rockville, Md.: National Institutes of Health, 1989.

———. "Alcohol Alert 10: Alcohol and Women." (pamphlet). Rockville, Md.: National Institutes of Health, 1990.

———. "Alcohol Alert 13: Fetal Alcohol Syndrome." (pamphlet). Rockville, Md.: National Institutes of Health, 1991.

———. "Alcohol Alert 16: Moderate Drinking." (pamphlet). Rockville, Md.: National Institutes of Health, 1992.

————. "Alcohol Alert 18: The Genetics of Alcoholism." (pamphlet). Rockville, Md.: National Institutes of Health, 1992.

————. "Alcohol Alert 19: Alcohol and the Liver." (pamphlet). Rockville, Md.: National Institutes of Health, 1993.

————. "Alcohol Alert 22: Alcohol and Nutrition." (pamphlet). Rockville, Md.: National Institutes of Health, 1993.

————. "Alcohol Alert 23: Alcohol and Minorities." (pamphlet). Rockville, Md.: National Institutes of Health, 1994.

————. "Alcohol Alert 25: Alcohol-Related Impairment." (pamphlet). Rockville, Md.: National Institutes of Health, 1994.

————. "Alcohol Alert 26: Alcohol and Hormones." (pamphlet). Rockville, Md.: National Institutes of Health, 1994.

————. "Alcohol Alert 28: Alcohol and Tolerance." (pamphlet). Rockville, Md.: National Institutes of Health, 1995.

————. "Alcohol Alert 31: Drinking and Driving." (pamphlet). Rockville, Md.: National Institutes of Health, 1996.

————. "Alcohol Alert 34: Preventing Alcohol Abuse and Related Problems." (pamphlet). Rockville, Md.: National Institutes of Health, 1996.

————. "Alcohol Alert 35: Alcohol and Metabolism." (pamphlet). Rockville, Md.: National Institutes of Health, 1997.

————. "Alcohol Alert 37: Youth Drinking: Risk Factors and Consequences." (pamphlet). Rockville, Md.: National Institutes of Health, 1997.

————. *Alcoholism: Getting the Facts.* Rockville, Md.: National Institutes of Health, 1996.

O'Brien, Robert, and Morris Chafetz. *The Encyclopedia of Alcoholism,* 2nd ed. New York: Facts On File, 1991.

Olson, Steve. *Alcohol in America.* Washington. D.C.: National Academy Press, 1985.

Rorabaugh, W. J. *The Encyclopedia of American Social History,* Vol. III. New York: Charles Scribner's Sons, 1993.

U.S. Department of Health and Human Services. *Ninth Special Report to the U.S. Congress on Alcohol and Health.* Washington, D.C.: U.S. Government Printing Office, 1997.

Woititz, Janet Geringer. *Adult Children of Alcoholics.* Deerfield Beach, FL: Health Communications, Inc. 1990.

APPENDIX

FURTHER READING

American Psychiatric Association. *Diagnostic and Statistical Manual of Mental Disorders*, 4th ed. Washington, D.C.: American Psychiatric Press, 1994.

———. *Treatment of Psychiatric Disorders*, 2nd ed. 2 vols. Washington, D.C.: American Psychiatric Press, 1994.

Babor, Thomas. *Alcohol: Customs and Rituals.* New York: Chelsea House Publishers, 1992.

Fishman, Ross. *Alcohol and Alcoholism.* New York: Chelsea House Publishers, 1992.

Goodwin, Donald W. *Alcoholism: The Facts.* New York: Oxford University Press, 1997.

Jaffe, Jerome H., ed. *Encyclopedia of Drugs and Alcohol.* New York: MacMillan Library Reference, 1995.

Kinney, Jean. *Clinical Manual of Substance Abuse.* St. Louis: Mosby-Year Book, Inc., 1991.

Lang, Alan R. *Alcohol: Teenage Drinking.* New York: Chelsea House Publishers, 1992.

Lender, Mark Edward, and James Kirby Martin. *Drinking in America.* New York: Macmillan, 1982.

McGovern, George. *Terry: My Daughter's Life-and-Death Struggle with Alcoholism.* New York: Villard, 1996.

O'Brien, Robert, and Morris Chafetz. *The Encyclopedia of Alcoholism* 2nd ed. New York: Facts On File, 1991.

Olson, Steve. *Alcohol in America.* Washington. D.C.: National Academy Press, 1985.

Woititz, Janet Geringer. *Adult Children of Alcoholics.* Deerfield Beach, FL: Health Communications, 1990.

APPENDIX

GLOSSARY

Alcoholism: A complex chronic psychological and nutritional disorder associated with excessive, compulsive drinking.

Antiseptic: An agent that inhibits the growth of microorganisms and thus prevents infection.

Blood-alcohol concentration (BAC): The level of alcohol in the blood, usually expressed as the percentage of grams of alcohol per milliliter of blood.

Cirrhosis: A chronic disease of the liver that results in decreased function of liver cells and increased resistance to blood flow through the liver. Cirrhosis is characterized by the development of scar tissue to replace those parts of the liver damaged by inflammation.

Delirium tremens (d.t.'s): A disorder resulting from withdrawal of alcohol after chronic heavy use, characterized by confusion, hallucinations, and intense agitation.

Detoxification: The process by which a person addicted to alcohol or an illegal drug is gradually withdrawn from the abused drug, usually under medical supervision and sometimes in conjunction with the administration of other drugs.

Distillation: A process by which the alcoholic content of a liquid is increased. In the distilling process, a slightly alcoholic liquid is heated to a temperature between the boiling point of alcohol and water, and the resulting alcohol vapors that rise are caught and condensed back to form a liquid with a higher alcohol content. Distilled spirits include whiskey, rum, gin, vodka, and brandy.

Fermentation: The decomposition of sugar into ethyl alcohol and carbon dioxide, essential to the production of wine or beer.

Fetal alcohol syndrome: A collection of problems that affect an unborn child, associated with the mother's consumption of alcohol during pregnancy;

these include growth deficiencies and underdevelopment of the central nervous system and other body organs.

Intoxication: the changes in a person's physical and mental state brought on by the presence of alcohol.

Liquor: A general term in the United States for alcoholic spirits.

Metabolism: The chemical changes in the living cell by which energy is provided for the vital processes and activities of the cell, or the process that uses enzymes to convert one substance into compounds that can be easily eliminated from the body.

Physical dependence: When a drug user's body has become so used to the substance that unpleasant physical symptoms will occur if he or she stops taking the drug.

Prohibition: The name given to the period from 1920 to 1933 when the manufacture, transportation, and sale of alcoholic beverages was prohibited by law in the United States.

Proof: A designation for the alcoholic strength of a spirit, indicated by a number that is twice the percentage of alcohol it contains. For example, a liquor that is 40 percent alcohol would be labeled 80 proof.

Psychoactive: altering mood or behavior.

Psychological dependence: The drug user has a powerful craving to use the drug, even if there is no physical need to do so (see **Physical dependence**).

Temperance movement: An organized drive against the manufacture, sale, and consumption of alcoholic beverages. In general, temperance advocates support moderate drinking, not total abstinence, although strong temperance movements that call for total abstinence have occurred at various times in U.S. history (most notably leading to the period known as **Prohibition** in the 1920s and '30s), as well as in other parts of the world.

Tolerance: The alcoholic's need for increasing amounts of the drug to achieve the same level of intoxication. Long-term addicts may develop such high tolerance that they can take amounts that would kill a non-user.

Withdrawal: The physical and mental symptoms that occur when a person who is physically dependent on alcohol stops drinking. Withdrawal symptoms may include muscle aches and cramps, fever, vomiting, and weakness, as well as mental symptoms such as depression and hallucinations (see **Delirium tremens**).

APPENDIX

INDEX

APPENDIX

PICTURE CREDITS

Senior Consulting Editor Carol C. Nadelson, M.D., is president and chief executive officer of the American Psychiatric Press, Inc., staff physician at Cambridge Hospital, and Clinical Professor of Psychiatry at Harvard Medical School. In addition to her work with the American Psychiatric Association, which she served as vice president in 1981–83 and president in 1985–86, Dr. Nadelson has been actively involved in other major psychiatric organizations, including the Group for the Advancement of Psychiatry, the American College of Psychiatrists, the Association for Academic Psychiatry, the American Association of Directors of Psychiatric Residency Training Programs, the American Psychosomatic Society, and the American College of Mental Health Administrators. In addition, she has been a consultant to the Psychiatric Education Branch of the National Institute of Mental Health and has served on the editorial boards of several journals. Doctor Nadelson has received many awards, including the Gold Medal Award for significant and ongoing contributions in the field of psychiatry, the Elizabeth Blackwell Award for contributions to the causes of women in medicine, and the Distinguished Service Award from the American College of Psychiatrists for outstanding achievements and leadership in the field of psychiatry.

Consulting Editor Claire E. Reinburg, M.A., is editorial director of the American Psychiatric Press, Inc., which publishes about 60 new books and six journals a year. She is a graduate of Georgetown University in Washington, D.C., where she earned bachelor of arts and master of arts degrees in English. She is a member of the Council of Biology Editors, the Women's National Book Association, the Society for Scholarly Publishing, and Washington Book Publishers.

In addition to *Drowning Our Sorrows: Psychological Effects of Alcohol Abuse*, **Nancy Peacock** is the author of *Alcohol* in the Chelsea House series JUNIOR DRUG AWARENESS. She has also written articles and columns for *BusinessWeek, New Choices, Midwest Living, Romantic Homes, Cleveland Magazine*, and many other periodicals, as well as travel books and a historical fiction novel. She lives in Medina, Ohio with her husband Larry and two children, Aaron and Natalie.